The London Loop

Colin Saunders

Aurum
Press.

Brimming with creative inspiration, how-to projects and useful information to enrich your everyday life, Quarto Knows is a favourite destination for those pursuing their interests and passions. Visit our site and dig deeper with our books into your area of interest: Quarto Creates, Quarto Cooks, Quarto Homes, Quarto Lives, Quarto Drives, Quarto Explores, Quarto Gifts, or Quarto Kids.

Acknowledgements

Many people have worked towards creating and developing the London Loop. On behalf of all those who will enjoy walking it in future years, our thanks go to Simon Walsh and Roger Warhurst for devising the idea, and to Alec Baxter-Brown, Graham Butler, Catherine Cairns, Gary Cliffe, Helen Cocker, David Dench, Bob Dunn, Alister Hayes, Linda Jedda, Paul Mitchell, Gavin Rose, David Sharp, John Stern, Jim Walker, Trish Wickstead and other stalwarts of the London Walking Forum and Strategic Walks Network, and officers of the various London boroughs and county councils, whose efforts turned it into reality. The author is also grateful to David Cockle, Des de Moor, Dr Alan Harrington, Cathy Sharp and the people in Transport for London's Walking Section for their help.

First printed in 2017 by Aurum Press
An imprint of the Quarto Group
The Old Brewery, 6 Blundell Street, London N7 9BH

This product includes mapping data licensed from Ordnance Survey® with the permission of the Controller of Her Majesty's Stationery Office. © Crown copyright 2017. All rights reserved. License number 43453U.

Ordnance Survey and Travelmaster and registered trademarks and the Ordnance Survey symbol and Explorer trademarks of Ordnance Survey, the national mapping agency of Great Britain.

A catalogue record for this book is available from the British Library.

ISBN 978 1 78131 561 3

1 3 5 7 9 10 8 6 4 2
2017 2019 2021 2020 2018

Book design by Carr Design Studio Ltd
Printed and bound in China

Cover photograph: River Thames and Kingston Bridge from Charter Quay
Title-page photograph: Narrowboat on the Grand Union Canal at Uxbridge

Aurum Press want to ensure that these trail guides are always as up to date as possible – but stiles collapse, pubs close and bus services change all the time. If, on walking this path, you discover any important changes that future walkers need to be aware of, do let us know. Either send us an email to trailguides@quarto.com or, if you take the trouble to drop us a line to:

Trail Guides, Aurum Press, 74-77 White Lion Street, London N1 9PF,

we'll send you a free guide of your choice as thanks.

Contents

How to use this guide

Some readers have told us that they like to follow the route in this guide, even though they have no intention of walking it! But if you do mean to walk it eventually, you should try to read the description beforehand so that you have an idea of what lies in store and to help plan your day. This applies especially if you are unfamiliar with walking in the countryside, or if you think certain types of terrain may be unsuitable for you.

Previous editions of the London Loop guide divided the route into 15 sections, but as the route is officially divided into 24 sections this caused some confusion, so for this edition we have fallen into line to use the official number. The guide is in several parts:

First by way of introduction, a brief account of how the London Loop came to be devised by the London Walking Forum, and the role played by Transport for London and its Walk London programme.

Second, some guidance on walking the route, and how to make best use of London's excellent public transport system to reach it.

Third, a complete description of the walk itself, divided into 24 sections, all of which start and finish at places with public transport. The route is illustrated with 1:25,000 maps, specially prepared for the Loop by the Ordnance Survey® from their 1:25,000 Explorer™ maps. With text and map on the same opening, you should find it easy to follow the Loop, whether or not its signs and waymarks are in place.

Reference points are used, both in the text and on the maps: by letters **[A]** for key geographical points; and by numbers **[1]** to indicate features of special interest. Other information of importance to walkers, such as public transport, pubs, cafés, toilets and good spots for picnicking are also identified.

Finally, the Useful Information section section tells you more about public transport and fares, organisations involved with walking in London, and a distance calculator.

Colin Saunders

Sadly, *David Sharp* died in April 2015. As well as being the original author of this guide, he was the chairman of the Orbitals Working Party of the London Walking Forum, which steered the development and promotion of the London Loop and its companion, the Capital Ring. The author of this new edition is most grateful to David for all his help and encouragement. His presence remains with us as most of the photographs in this edition are his, and several of his whimsical asides have been retained.

PART ONE

Introduction

A long stretch of the Loop through Bushy Park passes Heron Pond.

London is one of the world's greenest cities, and this becomes very obvious if you fly over it, either in an aircraft or on Google Earth. It gets greener as you move away from the centre, towards the Greater London boundary, where there are many public open spaces, lovely countryside, water features and even farmland. The 240-km/150-mile London Loop takes full advantage of this by weaving a route that lies mostly just inside the boundary, but occasionally strays into the neighbouring counties of Surrey, Buckinghamshire, Hertfordshire and Essex. The Loop has been described as 'the walker's M25', though always staying inside it, but of course we hope you will find this particular circumnavigation of the capital a much more pleasurable experience, at a pace that allows you to enjoy the many wonderful views and points of interest – and there should be no hold-ups!

Back in 1990, someone in the London branch of an organisation called the Countryside Commission (now Natural England) called a meeting to discuss how people could be encouraged to take advantage of the amazing opportunities that London presents for walking. It was attended by representatives of the London boroughs, the Ramblers' Association and other similar bodies, as well as individuals with an interest in the subject, including the author of this book! Out of this meeting was born the London Walking Forum, which was formally launched at the House of Lords in January 1993.

There followed a remarkable explosion of ideas for new walking routes, many

of which have since been created by London boroughs and other organisations, and the Loop shares parts of its route with many of them. But a more ambitious proposal was put forward: grand circular routes that would link most of the boroughs, requiring considerable inter-borough co-operation. One route should, like the M25, closely follow the Greater London boundary, and a second should follow a course about halfway in. Twenty-six London boroughs and four county councils came together under the co-ordination of the London Walking Forum to create these wonderful routes for walkers.

Competitions were held to decide on catchy names for these routes, and with little argument the inner circle became the Capital Ring, but the outer one proved more contentious. The winner of its competition was 'London Outer Orbital Path', which resulted in the appropriate acronym 'Loop'. But then it was proposed that the route should be marketed as 'London Loop', and many of those involved felt that this was a nonsense: the mixture of lower and upper case looked very odd, was awkward to write or type and indeed tautological, in effect 'London London Outer Orbital Path'. Furthermore, the Ordnance Survey and other bodies refused to use 'London Loop'. Although you may still see it, this format is rarely used now, and in this new edition of the guide we use 'London Loop', or sometimes just 'the Loop'.

Whatever the title, there's no argument about the great variety of walking that the Loop provides: woods, heaths, parks, fields, nature reserves, river banks and canal towpaths. Inevitably there has to be some linking stretches through suburbia, though this is nearly always on pleasant residential roads.

Walk London

The Walk London network was set up in 2005 (as the Strategic Walk Network) by Transport for London (TfL) and comprises seven high-quality walking routes that span the capital. They include the two Orbital Walks (Capital Ring and London Loop), Green Chain Walk, Jubilee Greenway, Jubilee Walkway and Lea Valley Walk, plus the Thames Path within Greater London. Information sheets for all these routes are free to download from the TfL website www.tfl.gov.uk/walking.

TfL provided £9 million of funding between 2005 and 2012 to raise those seven routes to a consistently high standard. They continue to be promoted by TfL and its partners through regular events such as the popular and free thrice-yearly weekends of led walks. At the time of writing, a new initiative to enhance and extend London's walking network was being developed, and further information will become available in due course on the TfL Walking website.

Reaching the London Loop

Most Loop walkers are likely to live in London or south-east England, and undertake the route in a series of day or half-day trips, divided into distances with which they are comfortable. To help with planning, a distance calculator is provided on page 159. Walkers from further afield may prefer to tackle the route as a major expedition, staying overnight,

Unmissable boards like this announce land owned by the City of London.

which could take one or two weeks or more. The most practical way of doing this would be to stay in central London and travel out and back each day using Oyster or a Travelcard. More awkwardly, living out of a rucksack but saving travelling time, accommodation along the route can be identified on Google or Bing maps by typing 'accommodation' followed by the place name in the search box.

Although it follows a vast, almost complete circle, the London Loop is, for practical purposes a linear walk of 240 km/150 miles. The great majority of users will be travelling out from their base in London or nearby, putting in a day's walking, then returning home from a point further along the circuit. The route is designed to pass by or close to stations, nearly all of them within Transport for London's zonal system, so walkers should find using public transport most convenient. In fact, the route passes or has links to 47 stations, and there are many bus routes in between, most of which have frequent daily services. Thus you can use your Oyster card or buy a Travelcard that will take you out and back with complete freedom to swap between Tube, Docklands Light Railway, most National Rail services and all London buses.

London's pensioners will know that their Freedom Pass gives them the same facility, though it cannot be used before 09.30 on most National Rail services (except on Saturdays, Sundays and public holidays).

The availability of public transport around the route is indicated in the text

and on our maps by the symbols ⇌ National Rail, ⊖ London Underground (the Tube), ⊖ London Overground, and 🚊 Tramlink. Bus services are indicated by the symbol 🚌 , followed by the names of stations served from that location. Oyster and Travelcards cannot be used on certain services outside Greater London, indicated 'non-TfL' in the text, in these cases you must pay the relevant fare. For further details see the Transport section on page 157.

Walking the London Loop

The London Loop is divided into 24 sections, ranging from around 6 km/4 miles to 16 km/10 miles and averaging 10 km/6.25 miles – they are so uneven because they must fit the main public transport opportunities. To cover the whole route, the logical starting place is of course the beginning of Section 1 at Erith Riverside, but there is no compulsion to follow the sections in progressive order; you can join and leave at any convenient point in any order. As the route is decribed clockwise here, it is easier to walk in this direction. Using the maps in this book, you could go anticlockwise, but you would have to reverse the written directions, which may not be easy, and signage was incomplete at the time of writing. And when you have completed the route, a free certificate can be downloaded from the TfL Walking website.

Although it is mostly within Greater London, the Loop is predominantly a country walk, often along typical country paths, and climbs to over 150 metres/500 feet at several places. It offers just about every type of walking: mostly paths and tracks that may be surfaced with grass, gravel, grit or earth – and the latter may be muddy after wet weather, but also canal towpaths, woodland walks and field edges. You will sometimes have to climb over stiles, though they are gradually being replaced by gates. The designers tried to make as much use as possible of open spaces and waterside, but inevitably there are places where the route has to follow roads.

One welcome advantage of walking in London is that you will never be too far from public transport (see 'Reaching the London Loop above) or other facilities such as pubs, cafés, and toilets, which are indicated on our maps by the symbols shown in the key found on the inside front cover. Pubs and cafés have toilets, but you should be prepared to buy something in order to use them. Places that have been identified by the author as potentially good spots for picknicking are identified by the symbol ✕ – this means there are several seats but not necessarily picnic tables, and somebody else may have bagged them first!

In urban locations you will usually be walking along roadside pavements. We show the names of all roads, streets or lanes that you encounter, although you may not see the actual name there. This is partly because some walkers take a street map and like to keep tabs on their location, and partly so that you can summon help if needed, whether a taxi or an emergency vehicle.

Most of the route is open 24/7, though you probably won't be walking in the

Hidden away in a grove of Petts Wood you may find this granite sundial memorial.

dark. Paths and tracks that are public are marked by green dashes on the maps – they could be closed at any time for maintenance or emergencies, but diversions should be signed. Riverside paths can sometimes be under water after heavy rain. A few parks traversed by the route close at dusk, and we draw attention to them in the text. Some stretches of the Loop follow what are known as permissive paths, as mentioned in the text, where there is no right of way but the landowner has given permission for them to be used by the public. In theory landowners are entitled to close them on one day a year – this is usually in the winter so unlikely to affect Loop walkers. If you find your way impassable for any reason, you should use the maps to navigate your way around the closure.

KEY MAP

London Loop

8 — Chapter Start Point

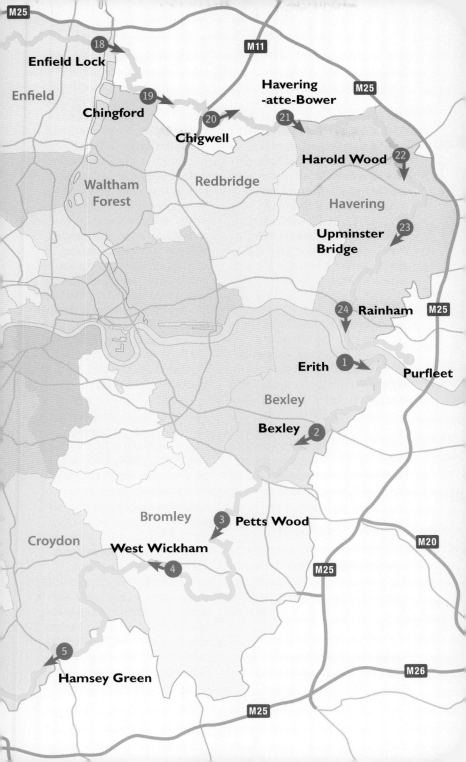

Accessibility. As so much of the London Loop goes through countryside, woodland and other open spaces on rough or narrow paths, with stiles, kissing gates, rough surfaces, ploughed fields and other encumbrances, the route as a whole is not accessible to wheelchairs or buggies. However, depending on individual circumstances and the type of conveyance you are using, some parts of Sections 1, 5, 11, 12, 17, 21, 22 and 24 may be suitable. Please read the route descriptions before setting out as they provide detailed information about the surface and terrain.

The route

Starting beside the River Thames in Erith, and expecting to head in a south-westerly direction, you may be surprised to find yourself first walking due east towards the North Sea! This is to gain access to the Cray Valley, which soon takes you in the required direction through Old Bexley village and the lovely Foots Cray Meadows. A long stretch through a series of woodlands follows, with very little urban interruption. Along the southern sector, the Loop follows a chain of commons that were saved by the forward-thinking Corporation of the City of London in the late 19th century for the enjoyment of ordinary folk. Skirting Kenley Aerodrome with its gliders, the route reaches its southernmost point in the aptly-named Happy Valley, near Old Coulsdon.

Swinging north-west now, the Loop mostly follows open countryside, straying into Surrey at Banstead Downs, Nonsuch Park and Ewell before joining the Hogsmill river into more urban surroundings to cross the Thames at Kingston. A long and delightful walk through royal Bushy Park, with a distant view of Hampton Court Palace, leads to another residential stretch through Fulwell and Hampton Hill. You are in green surroundings again beside the River Crane and on Hounslow Heath, but expect to be disturbed by aircraft approaching nearby Heathrow Airport. The towpath of the Grand Union Canal provides a pleasant change, accompanied by colourful narrow boats, with a diversion into Stockley Park, one of London's newest open spaces. The canal leads into and along the valley of the River Colne past idyllic Little Britain Lake and Uxbridge Lock, briefly popping into Buckinghamshire, to reach the westernmost point of the Loop at Black Jack Lock near Harefield.

Turning north-east, some glorious open countryside and woodland follows, much of it in Hertfordshire, passing W.S.Gilbert's Grimsdyke and the former RAF Fighter Command headquarters at Bentley Priory. Past Aldenham Reservoir, the Loop makes its way across the so-called Northern Heights, a hilly area of open countryside, making an awkward diversion to cross the A1 dual cariageway. Another watercourse, Dollis Brook, leads the Loop gently down to Barnet, then comes more undulating wooded countryside across Monken Hadley Common and Trent Park. The northernmost point of the Loop near Forty Hall in Enfield is reached along the valleys of Salmon's Brook and Turkey Brook.

Typical of many fine houses passed on the Loop, Forty Hall by Inigo Jones dates back to the 1630s and is now owned by Enfield Borough.

After crossing the broad Lea Valley, much of the Loop's north-easterly quadrant lies in Essex, starting through Epping Forest past Chingford and Chigwell then visiting the headquarters of the Scouts Association at Gilwell Park. The route continues across the Roding Valley, through Hainault Forest and Havering Country Park, with some prime Essex farmland in between. A series of streams is followed down the Ingrebourne Valley, through Harold Wood, Upminster, Hornchurch Country Park and Rainham village for the final stretch beside Rainham Marshes and back beside the Thames, passing an RSPB bird reserve to the finish in Purfleet.

As yet, there is no link back to the start at Erith on the far side of the Thames, so the Loop is not quite a complete circle but, in the strict definition of the word, a Loop!

Signs and waymarks

"Having firmed up the route, the next stage was to design signs to be used along it, but the choice of a logo led to arguments. What would best symbolise London's green spaces? The fox and the squirrel were early candidates, but loudly rejected with cries of 'Rodents! Pests!' by long-suffering countryside management teams. Finally the kestrel got the vote – the hunter you often see, if not recognise, hovering over the green areas of the Loop in search of prey." *David Sharp*

A variety of signs and waymarks indicate the route of the London Loop on the ground. In rural and other green locations such as parks and woodland, they usually consist of a simple plastic or metal disc, mounted on a wooden post. The disc has a white background and

contains a directional arrow with the kestrel logo in blue and the text in green. In a few places, there are two discs: the logo on one, the arrow on the other.

In urban locations, to avoid clutter, metal plates are strapped where possible to lampposts and other existing street furniture, but there are a few places where the Loop has had to be provided with its own special post.

At some junctions, fingerposts are used – usually they are plain affairs, where the Loop logo has been attached to the appropriate fingers, or the fingers bear the text 'London Loop'.

At key locations a much grander affair has been provided, which we call a 'Loop main sign': the wooden post has the location's name engraved into it, while the fingers have a plate inserted, showing distances to three other locations along the route in each direction. Information boards for the Loop often accompany these main signs, showing where it goes and how to get further details.

Sadly, signs go missing, or somehow mysteriously turn to point the wrong way, so you should not rely on them but follow the instructions in this book.

Some technical terms

You wouldn't think there was anything technical about walking – just placing one foot in front of the other until you reach your destination. Yet for many the London Loop may be their first close encounter with the countryside, and some of the terms used in this book may need explanation. A **bridleway** is a track that can be used by walkers, cyclists and horse riders – as distinct from a footpath, which is for pedestrians only. Whereas footpaths are indicated on waymark posts by yellow arrows, those for bridleways are blue. A **byway** is a track that is not quite a road, often with a soft surface, but can in theory be used by all traffic, though they are usually too narrow for larger vehicles. A 'restricted byway' cannot be used by mechanically propelled vehicles. The arrows for byways are red. A **kissing gate** is a contrivance with a swinging gate that can be used by pedestrians but not livestock. They are only found on footpaths, so should not be used by cyclists. A **stile** is a structure, usually made of wood but occasionally metal, which allows walkers to gain access to a fenced field or other enclosure, usually over a number of wooden steps. There should be a post to hold on to as you cross. They are only found on footpaths but are gradually being replaced by kissing gates.

Safety first

Not that we want to put you off! Those who regularly walk in the countryside will be very familiar with these circumstances and cope with them, but if this hugely enjoyable activity is new for you, it will be helpful to know what to expect. We have tried to draw attention to such hazards in the route description.

Busy roads. The route has been designed to minimise road walking, but inevitably much of it follows or crosses some busy roads. In this book, most of them can be idenitified by an 'A' or 'B' followed by a number. They are indicated in the route descriptions with a symbol. When crossing any road, common sense should prevail: you should only cross where it is safe to do so. Where possible, the route uses crossings that have some protection for pedestrians, but at some places a short diversion to a protected crossing is advisable. There are a few places where no protected crossing is available and extra care is required – it is hoped that these can be eliminated in due course. The route description sometimes suggests which side of the road to follow where this helps you to cross an approaching major road at a protected point, or reduces the number of road crossings.

Roads with no pavement. There are some stretches where the route follows roads that have no pavement, and extra care is needed. These too are indicated in the text with the symbol. ⚠ This is what the Highway Code advises in such situations: keep to the right-hand side of the road so that you can see oncoming traffic; be prepared to walk in single file, especially on narrow roads or in poor light; keep close to the side of the road; it may be safer to cross the road well before a sharp right-hand bend so that oncoming traffic has a better chance of seeing you; cross back after the bend. Additionally, wear something brightly coloured on top if you can.

Golf courses. The Loop crosses eight golf courses, where you should watch out for stray flying golf balls, especially when crossing a fairway. You may hear a golfer shout 'Fore!' if a ball is heading in your direction. Always allow golfers to finish their stroke if your passing might disturb their concentration.

Shared paths. Much of the Loop follows paths or tracks that can be used by both pedestrians and cyclists – this includes canal towpaths. Some are bridleways, which can be used by pedestrians, cyclists and horse riders. In urban locations, some routes have been specially prepared with a hard surface, with separate lanes for pedestrians and cyclists, but most have no demarcation. Cyclists and horse riders are instructed to give way to pedestrians, and when approaching from behind are supposed to call a warning or ring a bell, but regrettably some cyclists irresponsibly ignore all this, approaching from behind without warning and even using routes that are intended for pedestrians only. In return, when cyclists or horse riders approach, walkers are expected to stand aside to let them pass.

Trip and slip hazards. In some woodlands, tree roots can poke out of the ground. Some stiles are in a poor state of repair – you should test each step and post before putting your weight on it. Paving stones may be loose, and rabbit holes may be hidden. In wet or very cold weather some surfaces may be slippery, especially on the descent. Always try to take care, and you may find a walking stick or one or two walking poles helpful.

Barbed wire. In some rural locations farmers use barbed wire, either to keep livestock inside a field or to prevent walkers from gaining access into private property. It should be a safe distance away from the path, but there are some places where it is close

enough to cause injury or damage, especially if you slip. We have tried to provide a warning where this applies.

Overgrowth. Paths in rural areas can become overgrown, sometimes with stinging nettles and thorny plants. A walking stick or pole could be useful for bashing them down.

Animals. You may be delighted to see animals on your walk, and they add interest, especially for children. You should see deer in Bushy Park and horses at many grazing areas along the route. There are a few places where cattle or sheep are found, and they should not be a problem. However, animal behaviour can be unpredictable and you should keep clear, especially if cows have calves.

Walking with dogs. Always clean up any mess and keep your dog on a lead at roads, or under close control in parks, woodlands or open spaces, especially if livestock are present.

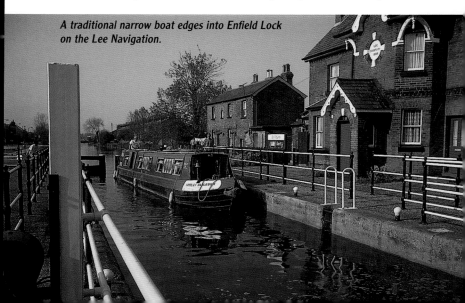

A traditional narrow boat edges into Enfield Lock on the Lee Navigation.

Historical and other points of interest

The author has tried to identify as many points of interest along the route as possible, but due to limitations of space it has not been practical to delve too deeply.

Much of the history is common to the whole area. From around 400 BC it was populated by Celtic tribes: the territory of four of them extended into the area now occupied by Greater London: the Cantiaci (Kent), Atrobates (Surrey), Catuvellauni (Hertfordshire) and Trinovantes (Essex). After the Roman invasion in 43 AD, the city we now call London was established as Londinium, most of the the local Celts became Romanised, settled there and built villas and small settlements on or near the roads out of Londinium.

After the Romans abandoned Britain in the mid 5th century, the Saxons soon occupied this area, absorbing or driving out the Celts. Even after the Norman Conquest in 1066, the Saxon names of most settlements persisted in modified form to the present day, as did those of what became the counties of Essex (East Saxons), Sussex (South Saxons), Middlesex (Middle Saxons) and Surrey (from 'Suthrige' – the south region of Middlesex).

Most of the Loop area remained farmland until the coming of the railways during the 19th century. This led to 'urban creep', a steady migration to more comfortable dwellings in what would henceforth be known as 'the suburbs' or 'the commuter belt'.

It is to the everlasting credit of more enlightened citizens at that time that so much open space was saved from housing development for the walkers of today. Most of the parks, woodlands and open spaces you pass through are owned by the appropriate London borough, or the district council where the Loop strays outside Greater London, though there are some exceptions as indicated in the text. Furthermore, much of the area through which the Loop passes is included in London's 'green belt', where urban development is banned or restricted, allowing the route to pass through open fields and farmland.

London has expanded steadily from the original 'square mile' of the Romans to absorb much or all of the surrounding counties. The River Thames provided the boundaries between Essex and Middlesex, to the north, and Kent and Surrey, to the south. Then in 1889 the County of London was created, covering most of the built-up area as it then was, to about 11 to 13 km/7 to 8 miles) from the city centre. But the inexorable creep of suburbia continued and in 1963 Greater London was formally created, absorbing the former counties of London and Middlesex plus parts of Kent, Surrey, Hertfordshire and Essex. Further development has had to 'leapfrog' the green belt to places further away, but there is considerable pressure to relax the restriction. For the sake of the London Loop and all opportunities for walking and other forms of quiet enjoyment, we hope that this pressure will continue to be resisted.

D-Day barges abandoned at Rainham Marshes

PART TWO

The London Loop

Erith to Bexley

13.4 km/8.3 miles, plus links 0.4 km/0.2 miles from Erith station and 0.2 km/0.1 miles to Bexley station. You can leave the route at Slade Green after 6.5 km/4 miles, Crayford after 10 km/6.2 miles or several bus stops as described.

Pubs, cafés and toilets at Erith, Crayford, Hall Place and Bexley. Best picnic opportunity at Crayford Waterside.

Local authority: London Borough of Bexley.

The Loop starts its journey by following three rivers in quick succession – Thames, Darent and Cray – and it's mostly easy, level walking on firm paths and tracks with just one stile. You pass the monstrous Darent Flood Barrier, then there's a charming interlude at Crayford's Waterside district, followed by long stretches of greenery through Hall Place Park, with its delightful mansion and gardens, and Churchfield Wood.

Link from Erith Station ⇌
(340 metres). From the handsome little station building **[A]**, turn right along the tiled approach road then swing sharp left with it under a flyover. At an odd cobbled roundabout, turn right along Stonewood Road, passing an entrance to Bexley College. At the end, keep left beside another roundabout – this one shaped like a teardrop – onto Walnut Tree Road. Cross at the refuge beside Tramway House and keep ahead past the name sign for Erith High Street into **Riverside Gardens** **[1]**, where you turn right to start the Loop. Ignore signs around here for the Green Chain Walk, which shoots off in a completely different direction.

Every walk should start with a grand gesture to send you on your way,

and the broad Thames estuary at Erith (pronounced Earith) meets this brief most emphatically. Though at the official starting point in Riverside Gardens you may wonder where it is! Follow the path through the gardens, with a great wind turbine beckoning, and passing a flagpole cunningly disguised as a yacht's mast, until you come to some steps **[B]** on your left, leading to a viewing platform. And suddenly there's the Thames, 0.8 km/0.5 miles wide here. The rolling downs opposite look so natural, but in truth they consist of grassed-over rubbish, and you will have a close encounter with them on the Loop's final section.

Loop signage in this area is combined with that of the Thames Path, whose route we share as far as Crayford Point. The Thames Path National Trail, established in 1996,

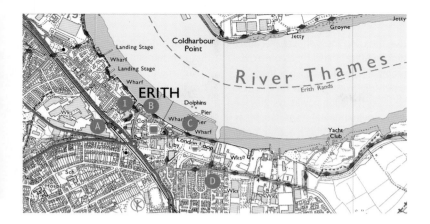

follows the river from its source near Kemble in Gloucestershire for 295 km/184 miles to the Thames Barrier, but a 17.5-km/11-mile extension that is not part of the national trail continues through Erith to join the Loop as far as the mouth of the River Darent. We also accompany National Cycle Route 1 as far as Barnes Cray: it is Britain's longest cycle route at 2,712 km/1,695 miles, linking Dover with the Shetland Islands.

Descend the steps and turn right along the William Cory Promenade, named not after the 19th-century poet but the founder of the company that operated tugs and colliers from London. It ends at a blank wall, beside a jetty from which a ferry used to cross the Thames. At present, Erith's riverside is fragmented by buildings, so you must turn right up a ramp, then left along the High Street, passing a trio of buildings with history: the former police station, the Cross Keys pub and the Playhouse theatre. Turn left between the pub and the theatre along a path that leads down flights of steps

and back to the riverside. Ahead now is what many now call 'Erith Pier' [C], though properly Deep Wharf, where ships use to discharge cargo, but now with full public access. What with the pier and the promenade, all it needs is some beach huts and Erith could claim to be a seaside resort!

Pass a long blue shed to the end of the promenade, with a vast Morrisons supermarket to your right. Turn right to cross Wheatley Terrace Road, then keep ahead between bollards along Appold Street and turn left beside busy Manor Road [D] for nearly 0.8 km/0.5 miles. Until such a time as the riverside here becomes available for public

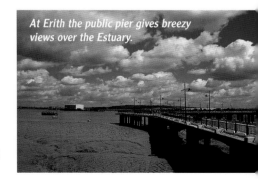

At Erith the public pier gives breezy views over the Estuary.

use, the Loop must endure this dusty thoroughfare lined with commercial premises, among which are many scrap-iron merchants, as they used to be known, though nowadays they gain some environmental respectability as 'metal recyclers'. Watch out for lorries and fork-lift trucks emerging from the sheds.

Eventually, just before Manor Road swings right, a great white wind turbine rears up to your left, and this no doubt essential hive of industry comes to an abrupt end. Turn left along the drive **[E]** of Erith Yacht Club, with the Cray Riverway joining our little band of trails – we shall follow its entire length of 16 km/10 miles. Follow the drive as it swings right, past some bollards, and when it turns left into the yacht club, keep ahead through a barrier to continue along a gravel track atop an embankment lined with wild flowers and aflutter with butterflies. You are now at last in open country, with the river and salt marsh to the left, grazing land to the right and the **Queen Elizabeth II Bridge [2]** ahead.

The Queen Elizabeth II Bridge is part of the Dartford Crossing. Opened by Her Majesty Queen Elizabeth II in 1991, it is a cable-stayed bridge whose 450-metre main span is supported by cables that run from two towers reaching 137 metres in height. In effect it is part of the M25 London orbital motorway, though officially categorised as the A282, where toll-paying traffic uses the bridge southbound and the Dartford Tunnel northbound.

Plod on to reach another, even larger community of metal recyclers occupying **Crayford Ness [3]**, a headland jutting into the river. The Thames Path comes to an abrupt end here, halted in its tracks by the River Darent, though there is a proposal to bridge the river mouth. On the far bank of the Thames now is Rainham Marshes Nature Reserve, and a little further on the little town of Purfleet, where the Loop reaches its own conclusion. Rising timidly from the metal-crunching mayhem is a gaunt, skeletal tower that supports a radar installation of the Port of London Authority.

The Loop continues around to the right to follow the meandering Darent, known here as Dartford Creek, where Greater London ends, with the county of Kent on the far side. You pass one of the 1,000 quirky Millennium Mileposts, all different, that were installed along cycle routes throughout the country, to reach the **Darent Barrier [4]**.

The Darent Barrier is properly called the Dartford Creek Tidal Flood Barrier, whose 'drop-leaf' gate can be lowered to prevent inundation of the hinterland. Sometimes written as 'Darenth', the river rises in the Greensand Hills near Westerham and flows for 34 km/21 miles to Dartford, continuing as a tidal estuary – **Dartford Creek [5]** – to the Thames at Crayford Ness.

Cross the barrier's access road and continue along the embankment for 1.2 km/0.8 miles to a junction with the fire-scorched remains of a knobbly seat

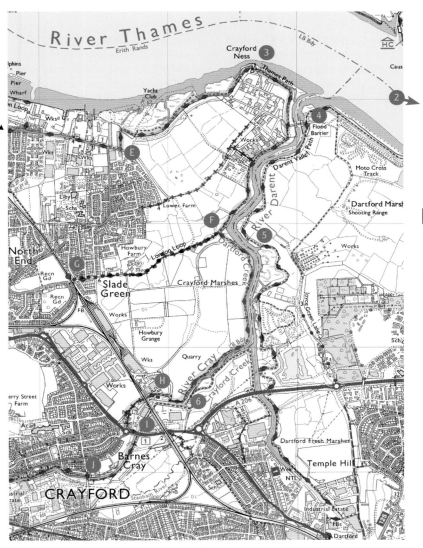

[F], where the river lurches leftwards. *The path that goes right here will take you in 1.2 km/0.8 miles to Slade Green Station [G].* The Loop stays beside the Darent for another 1 km/ 0.6 miles, the path much narrower now but still shared with cyclists, and with a long hedge on your right. The tall chimney that rises prominently

over to your left belongs to Dartford's Littlebrook Power Station, closed in 2015 and awaiting its fate.

A busy road and a power line have been threatening ahead, but before you reach them your progress is halted by another tributary, this time the River Cray, forcing you rightwards along **Crayford Creek [6]**. The River Cray rises from springs in Orpington and gives its name to a family of settlements hereabouts: Barnes, North, Foots, St Paul's and St Mary, as well as Crayford. A long, grassy mound on your right betrays its origin as a landfill site, occupying an old gravel quarry. As another tributary sneaks out of the far bank, this time the little Stanham River, the path swings right, through barriers and around a mobile phone mast to reach a dusty road **[H]** that serves a motley collection of yet more metal recyclers and aggregate producers in the Crayside Industrial Estate. Be warned: the tyrannosaurus rearing up on your left is actually a colossal aggregate loading machine.

Turn left on a fenced footway beside the road, dive under a railway line and follow the road round to the left, keeping strictly to the footway along the left-hand side. Take care as thundering great lorries use this road. At a fork, cross the road and keep ahead, but beware lorries approaching from behind. At the A206 Thames Road, cross the dual carriageway at the lights then go left and right beside a small side road to cross more lights to the left over Crayford Way. 🚉 *From the stop on your right to Slade Green and Erith.* Turn left beside a small playing field, where walkers should keep right on a shared use track.

Back on the A206 now, cross the Cray then, in a few metres, at a tall wooden obelisk **[I]** where cycle route 1 goes ahead, turn right to follow a gravel byway beside the river for 500 metres. It has changed dramatically since last

seen: willows overhang the water and lush vegetation crowds in. At Maiden Lane **[J]**, turn right, back over the river, then in 30 metres cross over to turn left along Barnes Cray Road. When the road swings right, keep ahead past garages and through a gate to follow a gravel drive known as Iron Mill Lane, now with the river on your left. A sad stretch this, where a relentless run of backyards ignores the pretty outlook at hand – at least in summer, when foliage masks the vast industrial estate and power lines on the far bank. Watch out for a couple of information panels attached to a fence on your right.

Soon after a track junction, beside some garages, go left along a narrow tarmac path, staying beside the river, and pass through two gates to reach Crayford Way again in Crayford's attractive **Waterside district [7]**. 🚉 *From the stop on your right to Dartford; from the stop opposite to Slade Green and Erith.* Turn left along The Parade (automatic toilet opposite) to the traffic lights, where the link to Crayford Station starts. Turn right over two crossings to a corner of the gardens.

Take a moment to reflect on the fact that you are now standing on the site of the actual Cray ford, used by the Roman Watling Street on its way from Londinium to Dubris (London to Dover). And it's worth making a diversion through a gate on your right to look around the pretty Waterside Gardens, where you may find it hard to resist visiting Lindy Lou's Tea Room – a pun on its origin as a public convenience! There are more cafés nearby, and real ale fans may wish to inspect the Penny Farthing Micro Ale House on the far side of the gardens, opposite the curving turquoise bridge.

Link with Crayford Station

≷ (0.5 km/0.3 miles). Before turning right to the gardens, turn left along Crayford Road for 200 metres through the busy town centre, passing a bus stop 🚌 for Dartford. Continue past the junction with Roman Road as far as a McDonald's (note the Edwardian clocktower) and go over a pedestrian crossing to continue along the far side. 🚌 From the stop on your right to Plumstead, Woolwich Arsenal, Slade Green and Sidcup. Turn right at the roundabout along Station Road, then in 80 metres bear

right along Station Approach, a footpath leading to Crayford Station **[K]**. **Returning from the station**, use the exit from Platform 1 and turn right along Station Approach, continuing along Station Road to the roundabout. Turn left but stay on this side of Crayford Road, keeping ahead over the double pedestrian crossing at Roman Way to reach the corner of London Road **[L]**, where you turn left to rejoin the Loop.

Turn left now over two more crossings. The first leads to an island with the Bear and Ragged Staff pub to your right, but unless you wish to visit it take the crossing to your left to the far side of London Road **[L]**, where you turn right. Immediately on your left is Tannery Gardens, with a panel about its colourful history. Yet another double crossing takes

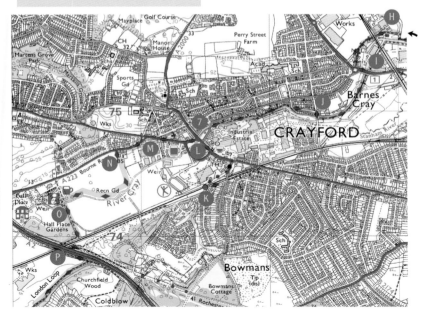

you over Roman Way to continue along London Road for another 250 metres, passing the Duke of Wellington pub. Bear left along a corner-cutting footway with a seating area into Bourne Road **[M]**. The industrial park on your left used to be the David Evans silk factory, one of the most famous of its kind, which operated here for 158 years from 1843 until it closed in 2001. A little further on is a motor showroom, where you should pay close attention to its forecourt: at each end is a slender column carved with shells and delicate ferns, left over from the time when they supported the canopy of Crayford Cinema.

Immediately after the showroom, turn left down steps and through a gate **[N]** into the main sports field of **Hall Place Park [8]**, a large public open space extending westward for 0.9 km/0.5 miles. Keep ahead across grass, staying 20 metres or so away from the left-hand boundary, to find a waymark post and a narrow path leading into the trees and back to our friend, the Cray. Follow the river for 320 metres to join a gravel path through trees into another field, still beside the river, and continue to a car park and sports pavilion **[O]**. *(If the riverside path is overgrown you can follow the field edge to your right on grass.)*

At the pavilion you can make a 250-metre diversion rightwards here, turning left past another car park to **Hall Place House [9]**, which has a café and toilets, with the Miller & Carter pub-restaurant next door.

Turn left across the river and briefly double back leftwards beside a hedge, following it round to the right into the 'flood plain field'. The beautiful gardens of Hall Place lie behind the hedge, but they are only accessible through the house. A footbridge takes you across an old channel of the Cray, though it may be dry, and on towards a railway line beyond a fence. Turn right with the hedge, along a grassy strip, and bear left at the end through a gate **[P]**. You will have become aware of a mighty roar of traffic by now, and a path takes you up 37 steps to face it – the dual carriageway A2 London to Dover Road, known here as the Rochester Way. You must turn left along the adjacent footway over the railway, but mercifully

The red-brick 1640s half of Hall Place looks across its gardens to the placid River Cray in Bexley.

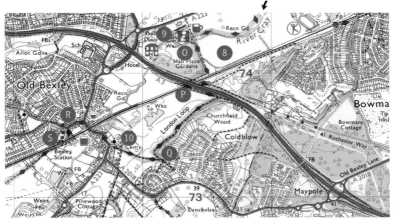

briefly as immediately afterwards you drop down a sloping path. At its foot is a junction, where you turn sharp left beside a fence.

This path takes you around two bends under the A2 to a fork, where you keep right, on the lower way. It has all the signs of being the original road, consigned not quite to oblivion by the new one that thunders past up to your left. As the old road starts to rise, turn right over a stile to take a path along the foot of a steep slope in Churchfield Wood, with an old fence on your right – watch out for some rusty barbed wire. In 0.6 km/0.4 miles the path bends left at some electricity junction boxes and rises to a squeeze barrier **[Q]** near houses. Turn right along a tarmac path, lined by lampposts and another barbed wire fence, which leads down past a cemetery and a path junction to Manor Road in Old Bexley. Opposite is the church of St Mary the Virgin **[10]**, whose odd shingled spire starts off as a pyramid but has an octagonal 'hat' topped by a weather vane.

Cross Manor Road and turn left around the church wall, then right into Bexley

High Street. Beyond the church, go over a zebra crossing to continue along the far side, but note the yellow brick High Street House of 1761 on your right, with its handsome portico – the home of John Thorpe, the 18th-century Kentish historian. Continuing along the High Street, you pass the Old Mill, actually a modern rebuild after a fire in 1966, which was a pub until recently. Not to despair – you will pass three more pubs and a couple of cafés as the High Street bends left, past the junction with Bourne Road and the handsome Freemantle Hall of 1894. Section 1 of the London Loop finishes at Tanyard Lane (Footpath 146) **[R]**, immediately after the Railway Tavern.

From the stops ahead: on the left to Eltham, on the right to Bexleyheath.

To continue on to Section 2 of the London Loop, turn left along Tanyard Lane.

Link to Bexley Station ⇌
(150 metres). Keep ahead past Tanyard Lane then immediately turn left up the station approach road **[S]**.

2 Bexley to Petts Wood

11.2 km/7 miles plus links 0.2 km/0.1 miles from Bexley station and 0.7 km/0.4 miles to Petts Wood station. You can leave the route at Foots Cray after 4 km/2.5 miles or Queen Mary's Hospital after 5.7 km/3.5 miles.

Cafés at Bexley and Petts Wood. Pubs at Foots Cray, Sidcup Place and Petts Wood. Toilets at Bexley and Petts Wood. Best picnic opportunities at Five Arch Bridge, Sidcup Place, Park Wood in Scadbury Park and (on a short diversion) the William Willett memorial in Petts Wood.

Local authorities: London Boroughs of Bexley and Bromley.

Continuing on level ground beside the River Cray, there's plenty of open space across windswept Old Bexley Conservation Area and the delightful Foots Cray Meadows. The route passes through Foots Cray village and climbs to Sidcup Place, then undulates through the ancient woodland of Scadbury Park, where you can view the remains of its manor house, before descending through Petts Wood. There are no stiles but towards the end you must cross three footbridges, each with 20-30 steps up and down.

Link from Bexley Station (150 metres). From the station exit **[A]**, turn right beside the approach road to Bexley High Street (cafés), turn right for a few paces then immediately right again along Tanyard Lane.

Follow Tanyard Lane as it bends right, between buildings and under the platforms of Bexley Station. The tarmac runs out here and the lane continues as a narrow (and possibly overgrown) path parallel with the railway for 180 metres. At its end, keep ahead beside a car park serving hockey and cricket pitches – the bar in the cricket pavilion is open to the public when there's a match on. Pass a row of cottages then climb a short rise leading through a gate **[B]** to a vast plateau known as **Old Bexley Conservation Area [1]**: previously a landfill site in an old

gravel working, it has been grassed over and is reverting to nature, with a kind of wild attraction.

Follow the grit path ahead to the far side, then descend an uneven and stony path through a gate underneath power lines. There's an odd little pocket of farmland on your right, and a water pumping station on your left, as the path leads on to join Riverside Road – something of a liberty, as the Cray is over 200 metres away at this point. Go ahead 50 metres, past the pumping station entrance, to find a footpath sign outside house number 106 **[C]**, where the Loop goes left. *If you need to break off here, though not an official Loop link, you can reach Albany Park Station [D]* ⇌ *in 0.7 km/0.4 miles by turning right up Betterton Drive to its end, then left along Longmead Drive.*

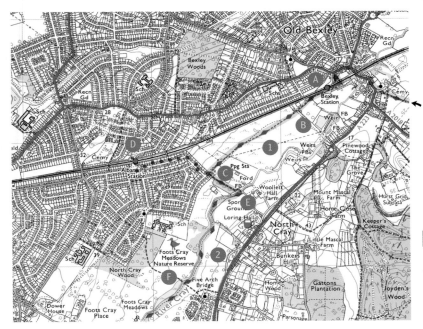

Go down the path, with the pumping station buildings on your left, back to the Cray. Cross it and turn right, through two gates **[E]**, to follow a riverside path with a fenced horse ride and a sports ground to your left. The narrow path leads past a footbridge to a point where the main path veers left through trees into **Foots Cray Meadows [2]**, the combined former parklands of North Cray House and Foots Cray House. The Loop stays right next to the stream – you need to tread carefully, as it is uneven in places, with exposed roots and can be muddy and slippery; at one point you must navigate through a sliced up tree trunk. If you don't fancy all that, you can take a parallel route along grass on your left most of the way. At a seat and fingerpost, continue beside the shallow river under two great weeping willows to reach Five Arch Bridge **[F]**, above a weir that has spread the waters of the

Cray into a lake, beloved of waterfowl. Several seats have been provided to sit and enjoy this lovely spot, while over to your left is North Cray's parish church of St James, though it may be hidden by foliage in summertime.

> "A perfect stretch of river scene this, with the clear water of the Cray burbling along over its gravel beds. The tranquil scene is marred only slightly by the distant rumble of traffic on the A223 North Cray Road, and an occasional screech from the ring-necked parakeets that have colonised the tall trees hereabouts." *David Sharp*

The Loop crosses a tarmac path and goes under another willow to resume its riverside progress for another 0.8 km/0.5 miles, briefly leaving the river at one point to cross a little wooden footbridge over a stream. Eventually, the path swings right, through a gate, to cross another attractive brick bridge [G], though this one has just a single arch. In 30 metres take a left fork on a narrow path beside a fence, then keep ahead at a path junction to reach a small grass area. Except when the trees are in full leaf, you should be able to see All Saints, the parish church of Foots Cray, on your right and a lilac-painted warehouse on your left.

Go half right on grass to a waymark post and pass between bushes to find on your right an information panel about the nearby church. Turn right, through bushes (may be overgrown) to a Loop main signpost [H] on Rectory Road, with the church to your right. One of those wooden obelisks appears, this time marking the end of the Cray Riverway, and although the river has flowed hither from its source a few miles south, we shall see it no more on the Loop. Turn left along Rectory Road, passing a width restrictor then Hope Community School (with its clock tower), a war memorial and the attractive Old House to reach the crossroads [I] in the centre of Foots Cray village. *There are food shops nearby, and the historic Seven Stars pub lies 230 metres to your left down the High Street.* 🚌 *From the stop to your left on this side to Bexley; from the stop to your right on the far side to Sidcup.*

Cross two sets of traffic lights – ahead then right – and turn left along the right-hand side of Cray Road. Take the second turning on the right, Suffolk Road, and its very end go left between fences and through a gate. The route follows tarmac paths for some way now. Bear left beside a playing field, then at

a junction [J] turn right through a gate and keep on between fenced-off horse pastures. At another gate, bear left past the end of a road, with the ground of Tudor Sports Football Club on your left. Keep ahead on a broad, twisting track between allotments, garages and garden fences then pass through a gate [K] into **Sidcup Place Park [3]**. Climb ahead through a belt of trees to the open parkland and continue upwards on grass, staying close to a line of trees on your right. Keep ahead to find a mown grass gap in the trees, and look back for a last look at the Cray valley. Go slightly right, closing in on a children's playground to join a crazy-paving path, then go left along it to a junction with a Loop fingerpost and information panel. Here now are the handsome red brick of **Sidcup Place [4]** mansion and its stable block.

Turn left along the tarmac garden terrace, where there are plenty of seats, with the ha-ha on your left. When the tarmac ends, bear half right on grass to pass two tall conifer trees, then between two shorter, light-green coniferous bushes, and on through a gap in the fence to A222 Chislehurst Road. 🚌 *To your left now is the bus station of Queen Mary's Hospital, from where buses go to Sidcup, Chislehurst and many other parts of south-east London.*

Cross over at the pedestrian lights, with Christ the King St Mary's Sixth Form College close by, then turn left along the far side. You now embark on an adventurous journey to get safely to the far side of a vast junction known as Frognal Corner, where the A222 intersects with the A20 Sidcup Bypass.

Start by diving rightwards down a shared-use track into a subway **[L]** (keep right), then climb a ramp on the far side (keep left) to cross a bridge over the roaring A20. Swing right to go down steps and through another subway (still keep left), then finally climb leftwards to reach the far side of the maze. Keep ahead beside the A20 for 30 metres then turn right through a gate **[M]** into **Scadbury Park [5]**. The Loop now traverses parks and woodland for the next 4.5 km/2.8 miles. Passing through the gate, you also crossed the boundary from Bexley into Bromley borough.

The well-worn paths in the park are of either earth (where you should watch out for exposed roots) or tarmac, much of which has broken up into ruts and loose stones. First follow the earth path ahead, then bear left at a junction between wooden railings to descend in woodland, swinging left then right to a junction. At the bottom, turn left across a belt of scrubland into a grove of magnificent redwood trees. Here you join the Friends of Scadbury Park's Acorn Nature Trail, marked by numbered posts (the Loop passes points 15 to 5 in descending order), which carry both said acorn and a QR code, so with the aid of a smartphone they will tell you more about the points you pass.

Climb the broken tarmac track past a barrier **[N]**, where it levels outs to continue between trees, with grassland on either side and a most satisfying vista to your right over the park's fields. You soon reach a junction, with a little pond on your left, and go slightly rightwards. Soon after passing post 13, which is on your right, turn left off the main track along a short, fenced earth path which links to another track. A tree trunk **[O]** here seems to have met obstructions that forced two ninety degree turns during its early growth. Continue down through the

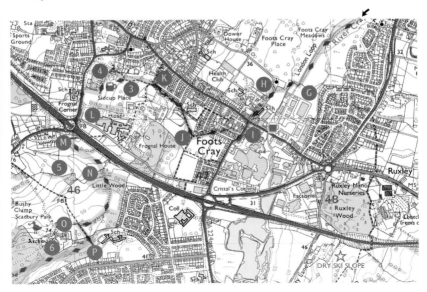

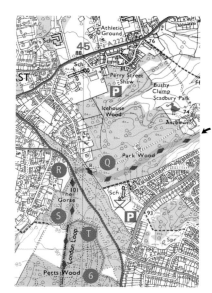

you turn right then left along a rough, stony, crossing drive to the A208 St Paul's Cray Road **[R]**. Briefly fork left across grass, then cross the road to a barrier and follow a track leading leftwards on to St Paul's Cray Common. In 40 metres take the left fork and press on along the track, passing a little patch of heather on your right, until you reach a major junction **[S]** by an information panel. Keep ahead into Petts Wood **[6]**, which is the name of both this group of ancient woodlands and the suburb ahead – the Petts were a family of 16th-century shipbuilders, who sourced their timber here.

In just a few paces, look out for a little 'National Trust Petts Wood' sign, where you can make an optional but worthwhile 120-metre diversion leftwards to see a granite column **[T]** to the memory of William Willett, staunch campaigner behind the Summer Time Act of 1925. Turn sharp left at the sign along a narrow, winding path through trees to reach a grassy glade containing both the column and a bench that would make a nice picnic spot for up to three people. Circling round to the back of the column, you will find a sundial, appropriately set to British Summer Time. If you forget which path you arrived by, it's the one to your right as you sit on the bench.

fine woodland to a junction with post number 12 **[P]**, where turn right to a fenced junction at the top of a rise, with signs saying 'Moated Manor', where the Loop continues ahead.

At this point, a brief detour to your right is highly recommended to see the remains of **Scadbury Manor** **[6]** with its moat. The path goes beside the moat and returns you to a point a little further on, where you turn right to rejoin the Loop.

Our route now follows a long track through Park Wood, still part of Scadbury Park, for about 0.9 km/0.6 miles, passing a raised dew pond on your right, and at last some seats. You pass a vast old oak beside some steps to reach a triangular junction, then continue for 30 metres to find post number 5. Turn left here along a path that passes through wooden posts **[Q]** to join another main track, where

Continue down the gently descending main track, ignoring waymarks for the wood's nature trail, for 0.8 km/0.5 miles, at first with open fields to your right, and those squawking parakeets overhead, for this is a stronghold of their quest to conquer Greater London. At a main junction, over to your right is another memorial stone **[U]**, this time for Francis Joseph Frederick Edlmann, who saved this part of the wood for us in 1927. Our track joins a broader one to reach another main junction **[V]** with a waymark post. Beyond it is a subway under a railway line but the Loop forks right here along a lesser path. Continue ahead at a crossing track and keep left at forks to stay near the railway line. Go over a plank bridge and down steps to come beside and then cross Kyd Brook, which gives its name to a London suburb further north and flows into the River Ravensbourne, which we encounter in Section 3. A timber causeway leads to a junction where you turn sharp left to cross a footbridge **[W]**.

The next stretch of the Loop is a trainspotters' paradise, as it crosses in short order a series of railway lines, all carrying commuter trains to and from London via Chislehurst Junction, away to your right. Our route uses three footbridges, all with 20-30 steps up and down, connected by tarmac paths. First is a tangle of four lines and points,

then a single branch line and finally a great spider's web of lines and points. Cross the first and second bridges, then a cul-de-sac called Little Thrift, and finally the third bridge to continue beside a metal fence to the end of Section 2 at a gate **[X]** on the edge of Jubilee Country Park.

To continue on to Section 3, keep ahead through the gate.

Link to Petts Wood Station
(0.7 km/0.4 miles). Turn left along the walkers' path, keeping right of a fence, to pass a car park and a National Grid depot, and join their drive into Tent Peg Lane. At the end, turn left along Crest View Drive to the main road, Queensway. ⛍ From the stop to your right to Bromley South, Bickley, Catford. For the station keep ahead along Queensway, passing ⛍ the stop for buses to Orpington, to find Petts Wood station **[Y]** ⇌ on your left. On the way you pass several cafés and J.D. Wetherspoon's Sovereign of the Seas pub.

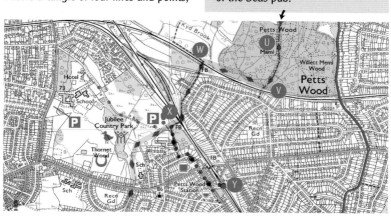

3 Petts Wood to West Wickham Common

13.2 km/8.2 miles plus links 0.7 km/0.4 miles from Petts Wood station and 1 km/0.7 miles to Hayes (Kent)* station. You can leave the route at Farnborough after 4.9 km/3 miles, Keston after 11.2 km/7 miles or several bus stops as described.

*This station is so named to distinguish it from Hayes (Middlesex), on Sections 10 and 11. In both cases, the distinction comes from their former counties before the establishment of Greater London.

Cafés at Petts Wood and High Elms Park. Pubs at Farnborough and Keston. Toilets at Petts Wood and High Elms Park. Best picnic opportunities at Tubbenden Meadow, Farnborough, High Elms Country Park and Keston Ponds.

Local authority: London Borough of Bromley.

The terrain gets quite hilly now, reaching nearly 170 metres/560 feet, mostly on rough footpaths in the foothills of the North Downs, with one stile. The Loop passes through several wooded areas, a country park and the first two of a string of commons owned by the City of London, as well as farmland. Keston Ponds is a delightful spot by the source of the River Ravensbourne, and there are historical associations with the Roman army and the abolition of slavery.

Link from Petts Wood Station

(0.7 km/0.4 miles). Take the Queensway exit **[A]** and walk past shops to turn right along Queensway, with several cafés nearby. Where the main road turns left, keep ahead on Crest View Drive, following it round to the left, then shortly turn right into Tent Peg Lane. A short way down, by the car park, go left on a path through trees, parallel with the lane and past the gate of a National Grid depot, to reach a meeting of paths **[B]**. Turn left past a gate to rejoin the Loop.

From the gate **[B]** follow the tarmac path into Jubilee Country Park **[1]**, named to celebrate the Queen's Silver Jubilee in 1977. After just a few paces go left on a stony path to keep near the edge of this attractive, heath-like area. The path curves leftwards, soon with a playing field and the buildings of St James Primary School visible on your left, except when the trees are in full leaf. At a gate, keep ahead along a narrow path, beside a fence and parallel with the school's driveway, to reach Southborough Lane **[C]**. From the stop on this side to Petts Wood and Orpington; on the far side to Bickley.

Use the zebra crossing to take Oxhawth Crescent opposite, then cross Chesham Avenue and continue ahead along Faringdon Avenue for 0.7 km/0.5 miles to its end, passing a grass roundabout **[D]**. You have now reached

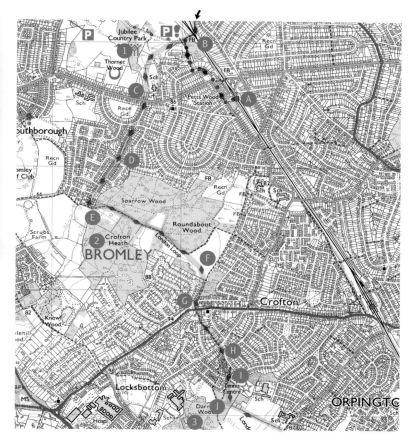

Crofton Wood **[2]**, a pleasantly wild tangle of birch and oak. Go sharp left on a narrow, stony path **[E]** beside a garden fence to join a broader path, deeper into the woodland and gently ascending for 1 km/²/³ mile, studiously ignoring all side turnings. Eventually cross a wooden footbridge then pass a bench seat to keep ahead at a triangle of paths to reach a junction with a tarmac track beside an information panel **[F]**.

Turn right past a barrier, bearing in mind that this is also a cycle route, to reach the A232 Crofton Road at a grass area **[G]** with seats beside

Crofton Brook. *125 metres to the left along Crofton Road: this side for Orpington and Petts Wood; far side for Bromley South and Hayes.*

Turn left past the village sign to cross the road at a pedestrian refuge, then come back a few paces to turn left up a narrow, fenced path beside the Crofton Oak Scouts and Guides Headquarters. It leads past the top of a road of bungalows to emerge at Lovibonds Avenue **[H]**, which you cross then continue along the road ahead (Crofton Avenue). In 100 metres ignore the first path signed to Farnborough, but another 75 metres further on,

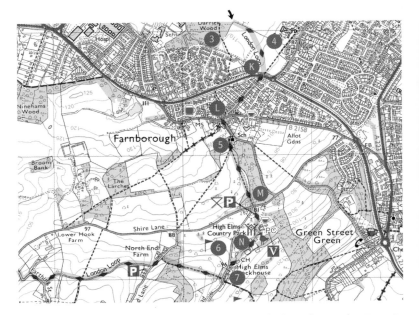

after La Tourne Gardens **[I]**, turn right at another path, similarly signed, into Darrick and Newstead Woods Nature Reserve **[3]**. At a junction, keep ahead beside a short wooden fence, then at the next junction **[J]**, with a fingerpost and an extended family of wooden fences, turn left between two of them, now in Darrick Wood.

Shortly, you'll reach another junction. Turn left then immediately right, along a track that briefly has two carriageways, with tennis courts to your left and a playing field to your right. It comes out unexpectedly at the top of sloping Tubbenden Meadow **[4]**, an excellent spot for a picnic with a view south towards the woodland of High Elms Country Park, soon to feature on our itinerary. Bear right on a grit path then drop down between an information panel and two seats to pass waymark post number 3 of the local nature trail. Take the mown grass path leading a

quarter right down the meadow to post number 4, and turn left beside a hedge, still within the meadow.

Go down three steps to a fingerpost then turn right along a causeway path, over what is usually a dry stream bed, leading to a footway beside the dual carriageway A21 Farnborough Way **[K]**. There is no protected crossing here, so go right a little to a dropped kerb and cross via the central reservation with great care. Keep ahead between a fence and a bush along a brick path past houses to reach a road. Cross it and continue along Gladstone Road to reach B2158 Farnborough High Street **[L]**, passing Pitt, Palmerston and Peel Roads – a prime ministerial theme is apparent here. 📖 *This side for Orpington, Sevenoaks, Tonbridge and Tunbridge Wells; far side for Bromley South and North, Shortlands, Eden Park, Anerley and Crystal Palace. There are food shops and a café to the* *left, while the Change of Horses and Woodman pubs are to the right. There is no public toilet in Farnborough, but members of the public are welcome to use the facilities of the Woodman pub during its opening hours, 200 metres to the right along the High Street.*

Turn right to the bend then cross over to the island. Follow the right-hand side of Church Road, which is lined by some fine old cottages. Continue along an elevated footway with a railing, which leads through a lych gate into the churchyard of St Giles the Abbott **[5]**. Go right of the church, past the ancient yew tree, and keep on into Church Field, a vast public open space. Walk down its left-hand side to reach woodland, down a few steps and follow a broad, stony path through barriers to reach Shire Lane **[M]**, at its junction with High Elms Road. You must cross this busy road with great care to take the path opposite, as traffic comes fast around bends from both directions.
📖 *A 'hail-and-ride' service stops anywhere safe near this junction, going left to Orpington.* Follow the short path through trees to a car park in **High Elms Country Park [6]**.

Follow a fenced path along the left-hand side of the car park to reach a tall, roofed information panel beside a barrier, with some picnic tables over to your left. Keep ahead on a broad, tarmac drive to a crossing path, where the Loop turns right.

It's worth a brief diversion here, up through a gate into the Bromley Environmental Education Centre at High Elms (BEECHE).

As well as the Green Roof Café, so named because it is constructed of environmentally friendly materials, there are an apiary, a wildlife pond, a wildflower meadow and a herb garden.

Passing some boulders, you are now following the original avenue that led up to the mansion, and you can see where it continued ahead between trees, though now grassed over. Stay on the tarmac as it winds up past the Eton Fives court *(toilets in the adjacent stable yard)*.

Continue around a clump of grand old pines to reach a parking area **[N]**. Turn right over an apse-shaped brick floor to head out across some landscaped terraces. This was the site of a great mansion owned by the Lubbock family which tragically burned down in 1967. You pass through what were its kitchens, then between two low stone columns to descend a grassy, conifer-lined path. At the bottom, go through a gate into the car park of High Elms Golf Club, skirt its left-hand side, passing the club house, and when its drive swings right, keep ahead between some notched posts and along a short dirt track to reach High Elms Road. Cross over to go through a fence, then immediately turn left along a path that runs parallel with the road and through the rather wild Clockhouse Community Orchard. On your left now, over the road, is the clock tower **[7]** that gives Clockhouse Farm its name.

Just past the Clockhouse, turn right up a track, watching out for exposed roots, to reach a meeting of tracks, where you keep ahead into a belt of trees between golf fairways. At a crossing track with a barrier, descend ahead to North End Lane. You must turn left along it beside the wall of North End Farm **[O]**, taking care as there is no footway. In 90 metres, turn right up an ancient, sunken green way with the intriguing name of Bogey Lane, which the Loop follows for 350 metres to a meeting of ways **[P]** by some steps. *You can stay on the lane if you wish, but it can get muddy in places and there's no view, so most walkers prefer to go up a few steps to follow a permissive parallel path in the field on your left, with a view across fields. Follow the field edge as it swings left, then when it does so again, more sharply, turn right through a gap in the hedge (it may be overgrown) and down steps to rejoin Bogey Lane at the meeting of ways **[P]**.*

Ignore path number one, going sharp left, and path two, leading into another field, and take path three, which dives into a belt of trees between fields. This leads to Farthing Street, another quiet lane with no footway, where you turn right, watching out especially for approaching vehicles at the right-hand bend as you wind down to meet Shire Lane **[Q]** again. It's no less busy than before, with fast traffic coming around bends both ways, so cross carefully to a fence that marks the start of a fenced permissive path going left, thoughtfully provided to take you off the parallel lane. Watch out for barbed wire.

Magnificent **Holwood House** **[9]**, now containing apartments, stands proudly to your right on

the site of an earlier building that was the home of William Pitt the Younger, prime minister of Great Britain during the late 18th and early 19th centuries. It was the location of an Iron Age fort, said to have been used by Julius Caesar's invading Roman army in 55 BC.

Soon a low stile turns you away from the lane to angle around trees surrounding Holwood Farm. The path leads to the farm entrance **[R]**, where the Jack Frost Pet and Country Store sells cold drinks and ice cream. *If you fancy something more substantial you can visit nearby Holwood Farm Coffee Shop, but to reach it you must tackle that Shire Lane once more, crossing it to walk 50 metres ahead along New Road Hill (signed Christmas Tree Farm), and watching out especially for traffic coming fast from the right. In New Road Hill, ignore the stop on your left, pass the coffee shop and continue a little further to the stop on your right, for Bromley South.*

The Loop continues by turning right at the farm entrance, through a barrier, along a tree-lined path, which climbs ever more steeply between fields. Before you enter the woodland at the top, look back for a last sweeping view over the vast swathe of open country that, almost unbelievably, is still within Greater London. Cross the drive **[S]** of Holwood House at its entrance gate, go through a barrier and keep climbing, to arrive breathlessly at the remains of the **Wilberforce Oak [10]**, one of the Loop's highest points at 169 metres/555 feet.

The Wilberforce Oak was the scene of a conversation in 1788 between William Wilberforce and William Pitt the Younger (see above) that resulted in a parliamentary bill to abolish the slave trade. They met beneath this already ancient tree, of which today only a hollow stump remains. A successor that was planted inside the stump blew down in the Great Storm of 1987; a second replacement has been planted nearby, though this will take centuries to bear the same gravitas.

Progress is easier now, as the route continues on the level for 500 metres to reach the busy A233 Westerham Road [T]. Cross over, slightly rightwards, to take a footpath – ignore the bridleway slightly leftwards. Keep ahead 20 metres, then turn right at waymark posts to go down a stony path in trees, passing a dingly dell, a grassy glade

and a timber revetment, to reach a car park. Follow its right-hand side to the entrance then go left a little to descend some steps to **Caesar's Well [11]**. At the time of writing there was a short signed diversion here awaiting repairs to the steps.

On the far side of the 'well', go left along the right-hand bank of the first of Keston Ponds **[12]** to reach a tall Loop fingerpost. Turn left along the dam between ponds, then descend steps to follow the left-hand side of the second pond to Fishponds Road **[U]**. There are seats and a picnic table here, and sometimes an ice-cream van. *Turn right along the lane, which has no footway, for 170 metres to Westerham Road. From the stop on this side to Orpington, Bromley South, Bromley North and Catford Bridge.*

Look for a '30' speed limit sign and cross there to a narrow path opposite.

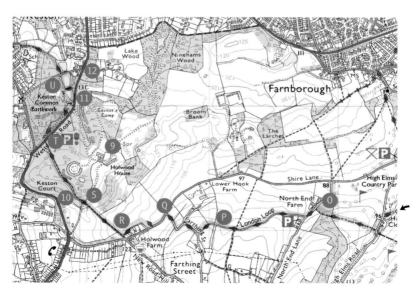

It joins a main path, which you follow, now with the third pond down to your right, and bends left to cross a couple of streamlets. Ravensbourne Meadows lie to your right as you climb gently to a junction. Ignore the bridleway to your right and keep ahead to join a tarmac path beside a green mesh fence and pass between Keston Primary School and a playground. At the end is Lakes Road **[V]** in Keston village, and you continue along it to reach the B265 Heathfield Road. Turn right, with the post office stores and the Fox Inn opposite, to a mini-roundabout **[W]**, where the Greyhound pub lies just around the corner. *From the stop on the far side to Bromley South, Bromley North and Hayes (Kent).*

At the roundabout, cross to the left over Heathfield Road, via a refuge, then turn right across Fox Lane and keep ahead on a roadside path to another roundabout at the junction of West Common Road and Baston Road. Confusingly, this is part of Hayes Common **[13]**, though Hayes itself is well to the north-west. The Loop now follows a woodland strip, roughly parallel with roads, all the way to the end of this section. In a few paces turn left down a track, but as it starts to bend right turn sharp right along a narrow path into trees, parallel with the road, watching out for exposed roots. In 300 metres the path comes back to the road and forks with it along Baston Manor Road **[X]**. The present manor is fairly modern, but in 1964 an important Neolithic site dating back some 3,500 years was discovered here.

The route dives back into trees and across the drive of Hast Hill House to reach a tall Loop fingerpost, which announces that you have arrived at West Wickham Common **[14]**, though the end of this section is still 1 km/0.6 miles away. Continue beside a fence, back in the trees, to pass a house called Midwood and rejoin the road, though by now it has become the A232 Croydon Road. *From the stop on this side to Hayes, Bromley South and Bromley North.*

Ignoring a sign to Hayes Station (this is not the Loop link), cross a side road **[Y]** (Hartfield Crescent) and keep ahead on a tarmac path between fences, which leads past a small car park. The Loop now follows a grit easy-access trail for 400 metres. It forks left at house number 91, then swings rightwards beside an area of restored heathland, bringing a little pocket of heather, bracken and mountain ash to the suburbs. At a blasted oak, keep ahead to carefully descend a steep and rough path of stone and sand – beware some well exposed roots. Continue past a junction to reach Gates Green Road, with Croydon Road to your right again. Standing tall here is one of the City of London's great, black-painted information panels. Go down to a gate and cross Gates Green Road to the opposite corner **[Z]**, where Section 3 of the London Loop ends. *Ahead along Croydon Road is Coney Hall Village, which has a café and food shops. From the stop on this side to Hayes, Bromley South and Bromley North.*

To continue on to Section 4, turn left along Gates Green Road.

Link to Hayes Station (1.1 km/0.7 miles). Cross Croydon Road at a refuge, to the corner of Coney Hill Road, turn right via another refuge and keep ahead, so that you are going back up Croydon Road beside a railing. In 80 metres cross the entrance into Nash College and go past its sign to turn immediately left up a narrow tarmac footpath called Polecat Alley. This leads you on a merry switchback for 250 metres to the entrance **[AA]** into The Warren, a Metropolitan Police sports ground. Ignore the public footpath that goes beside its fence; instead take a gravel byway to its left beside a house, Warren Wood Close – signed 'Sat Nav error'! At a gate, continue on a dirt track in trees to reach Warren Road **[AB]**. Keep ahead beside another part of Hayes Common then shortly turn left down Station Hill, past the junction with Ridgeway and on to the next junction. Cross right, via a white-painted area, past the New Inn and immediately left over the central reservation of dual carriageway Station Approach to Hayes station **[AC]** ⇌. There's a Costa coffee shop opposite and food shops nearby.

4 West Wickham Common to Hamsey Green

13.2 km/8.2 miles plus link 1 km/0.7 miles from Hayes (Kent) station. You can leave the route at Coombe Lane tram stop after 6.7 km/4.2 miles or several bus stops as described.

Cafés at Hayes, Coney Hall Village and Hamsey Green. Pubs at Shirley Hills, also Farleigh (0.8 km/0.5 miles off route). Toilets at Hayes station. Best picnic opportunities at Addington Hills viewpoint and Farleigh Common.

Local authorities: London Boroughs of Bromley and Croydon, Surrey County Council (Tandridge District).

Through woodland in the foothills of the North Downs, including more commons owned by the City of London. The going is generally fairly level, mostly on rough footpaths and on grass, with two stiles, however there are some rather steep ascents, reaching 150 metres/500 feet or more, and several long flights of steps. You cross the Greenwich Meridian, enjoy a great view from Addington Hills and visit the lovely gardens of Heathfield.

Link from Hayes (Kent) Station
(1.1 km/0.7 miles). There are toilets at Hayes station, a Costa coffee shop opposite and food shops nearby. From the station exit **[A]**, cross the dual carriageway of Station Approach via the central reservation, then turn right and left around the New Inn. Go up Station Hill, forking right with it to the top by Hayes Common. Turn right along Warren Road, then at Hillside Lane go left of a barrier and along a path into trees. Pass a gate and continue along unmade Warren Wood Close between houses. At Holland Way **[B]** and the entrance into The Warren, go straight ahead on a fenced path (Polecat Alley) as it falls and rises to join the A232 Croydon Road. Turn right beside a railing, cross

Coney Hill Road via one refuge, then go left over Croydon Road (another refuge), with Coney Hall Village down to your right. Keep ahead along Gates Green Road **[C]** to rejoin the London Loop.

From the junction with Croydon Road **[C]** walk 45 metres along Gates Green Road then turn right through a barrier along a tarmac path between houses and past a car park. Cross Kingsway *(café and food shop to your right)* and keep ahead up Church Drive to its end. Go through the gate into **Coney Hall Park [1]** and keep ahead on a broad tarmac path to reach a little Dalek-like pillar, which proudly announces that you are crossing the Greenwich Meridian – 'prime meridian of the world'. Continue past a pavilion and out of the park to go over Layhams Road at a zebra crossing.

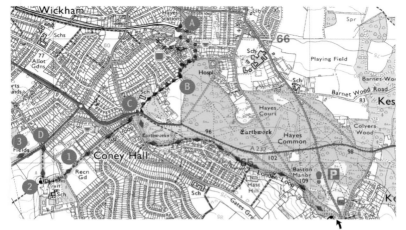

Keep ahead on a tarmac path, which winds around a disused car park and sports courts, then continues beside circular brick planters. Over to your left is Wickham Court, a 15th-century red-brick manor house with tall chimneys, but youthful voices may betray its current use as a school.

Ahead now is **St John's [2]**, the hilltop parish church of West Wickham – they seem to ignore 'the Baptist' these days. Pass through its lych gate then immediately turn right between

graves and drop down a few steps into Church Field. Cross it ahead down a well-worn grass path, noting the tree-shrouded hill to your left – that's Threehalfpenny Wood, where you will soon be walking. Go through a kissing gate to a roundabout on the A2022 Addington Road **[D]** and cross it at the refuge to your left. Turn left a few paces to go through an aluminium gate into **Sparrows Den [3]**, the home of Beccehamians Rugby Football Club, whose pitches stretch leftwards for 500 metres.

The Loop follows an ancient and well-trodden church path up to St John the Baptist parish church of West Wickham.

Follow the right-hand side, beside a hedge, to the car park then turn left, heading for a tarmac path that starts between the pavilion and another building, which houses a snack bar. Keep ahead past a crazy golf course and several seats, following a fence to its end. Bear right on an earth path into **Spring Park Woods [4]**, first of the woodlands on that hill you saw earlier, all owned by the City of London – and here's another of their huge boards! Guided by two lines of felled tree trunks, take the right-hand path. It climbs quite steeply, but not for long, and there's relief at the top when you turn left on to a crossing path of sand and gravel, because you can follow it on the level and in the same direction for a little over 1 km/½ mile, ignoring all crossing routes.

You have now entered Cheyne Wood, where an information panel tells the story of the Ancient Order of Froth Blowers. Soon after a fenced enclosure you reach a fingerpost **[E]**, which announces your arrival into Threehalfpenny Wood – and

coincidentally the London Borough of Croydon. Plod on, watching out for exposed roots to reach a major junction, where you keep right and climb a little over a crossing path. At the next junction, turn left into the open grassland of **Shirley Heath [5]**, keeping to its left-hand side at first. After following two waymark posts through a belt of trees, and with a fence over to your left, go right for 30 metres then turn left along the rightmost of two mown grass paths across another grassy area, with houses away to your right.

Dive back into trees to find a tall Loop fingerpost looming ahead at a junction **[F]** with a broad and well-used track, the Waterlink Way, where you should watch out for cyclists hell-bent on getting from London to Eastbourne or vice versa. Turn right along it for 170 metres to find a shorter fingerpost which turns the Loop left up a low embankment. Follow this narrow path and turn left at a junction, with more houses through trees on your right. You now need to concentrate at four forks:

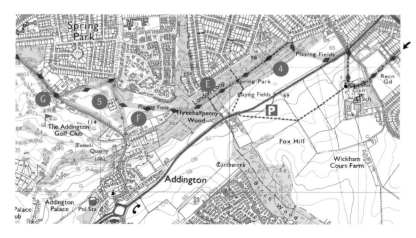

keep right at the first two, left at the third and right again at the fourth, then immediately turn right to reach Shirley Church Road **[G]**. Turn right again across Springhurst Close and follow the roadside footway for 500 metres, passing Foxes Wood on your right.

At the first house on your left, cross over at the refuge and continue down the left-hand side past the Pinewood Scout Centre to a mini-roundabout **[H]**. Follow the road as its bears left, still Shirley Church Road, past another roundabout and over Pinewood Close. Over to your right now is Shirley Church Recreation Ground, and way beyond it, if not too misty, you should see the Crystal Palace TV transmitter, The Shard and skyscrapers in the City of London. In 200 metres, with a children's playground **[I]** and tennis courts over to your right, go left on a tarmac path in trees beside the green mesh fence of Shirley High School. Soon turn right with the fence – it leads unerringly to Sandpits Road, and this in turn takes you to the busy Shirley Hills Road **[J]**, beside the

Sandrock pub, and there's another pub, the Surprise, a little way down to your right. *From the stop on this side to Addington Village tram stop; on the far side to East Croydon, Norwood Junction and Purley Oaks. The 19th-century Shirley Windmill [6] lies 250 metres down to your right – it is being restored and is open to the public on a limited number of days.*

Cross Upper Shirley Road, turn right then immediately left down Oaks Road, using the left-hand verge. In 130 metres turn left through a gate and into the woodland of **Addington Hills [7]**, then in 25 metres turn right along a rough earth path, which undulates and winds along, roughly parallel with the road. Turning away from the road, the path swings right across a small clearing and between some grand old oaks and hornbeams. It soon goes left again to climb quite steeply up a gravelly mound ahead and through gorse bushes to the viewpoint **[K]** at the top. You will no doubt wish to rest awhile here to admire the amazing view, and perhaps stop for a picnic, provided you don't mind hard

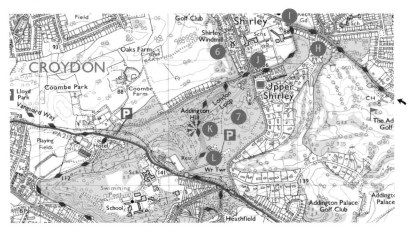

From Bramley Bank the Loop drops down the open ground towards Littleheath Wood, one of Croydon's attractive green spaces.

stone seats, and nobody has beaten you to them!

Having had your fill of the view, tear yourself away, go down the steps and keep ahead along a broad gravel path among trees and heather, which leads to the car park, but just before this on your right is the rather incongruously situated Royal Garden Chinese Restaurant **[L]**. At its near corner, lurking beneath the branches of a pussy willow tree, stands a Loop main sign, and you turn right there, along a gravel path beside a fence. It soon forks right, through a grove of majestic Scots pine trees, and on into a dip, wherein stands a lone and sadly dead three-limbed pine – give it a wide berth as it has been shedding branches.

Beyond the dip, keep ahead to a junction and turn left to the Coombe Lane Tramlink stop **[M]**, taking great care as you cross the tracks as the trams make little noise: look right over the first track, and left over the second.

From this side to Addington Village Interchange; far side to East and West Croydon and Wimbledon.

The Loop continues on the far side of the tracks through an array of fences, then bears left on a tarmac path, which goes through trees between the tramlines and A212 Coombe Lane. Continue to some traffic lights, which give the trams priority over road traffic, and cross over to the right. On the far side, turn right a few steps then go left through a gateway into the gardens of **Heathfield [8]** beside its lodge. Immediately after the lodge, go left along a shady path, a veritable tunnel of shrubbery. Soon descend 41 well-spaced steps, heeding the warning that they may be slippery when wet, to emerge at a most delightful spot around a duck pond.

Over to your left is Heathfield mansion, and it's worth making a short diversion past it to admire both the magnificent giant redwood tree on the lawn, and the view southwards over open countryside, marvelling that much of it is within the London Borough of Croydon!

Go clockwise around the pond, past the stable block, and now you must climb the same number of steps, forking right after the first seven, to leave the gardens through the car park. Go under the height limiter at the exit **[N]** and turn left down Riesco Dive, using the pavement on its right-hand side. Pass charming Clare Cottage at the bottom, on a farm track, but when this swings left keep ahead through a gate into

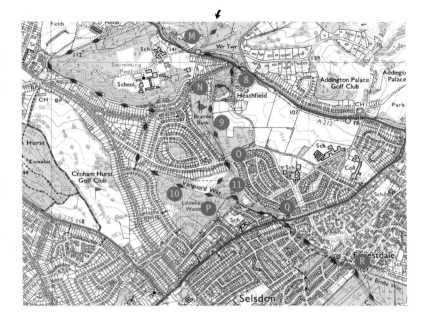

Bramley Bank [9], a nature reserve managed by the London Wildlife Trust. Take the left fork past an information panel to follow a path that undulates along, just inside the woodland edge, before climbing over the bank itself. Over the top, drop down through a gate to a broad grass area **[0]** linking two roads. 🚌 *Over to your left is the little St Francis Church, from where buses go to Addington Village tram stop.*

The Loop continues ahead, but a railing is in the way, so bear right to its end, beside a gate, then go round and back left up a tarmac path a few paces to continue rightwards over more grass. Go between some posts and past a tall information panel, with a house on your right, into **Littleheath Woods [10]**, an area of ancient woodland owned by the London Borough of Croydon and managed by the Friends of Littleheath Woods. In 40 metres you

must turn right at a fence corner, but mind the hole. Drop down into open grassland and follow a mown path along the middle, passing under some power lines. Take a left fork to keep a group of birch trees with some log stools on your right, then keep ahead back into woodland, to be greeted by a tall fingerpost **[P]** serving both the Loop and the Vanguard Way, which comes in from the right here on its 106-km/66-mile course from Croydon to Newhaven – the two routes run together for the next 3 km/2 miles.

Turn left up a track (a permissive bridleway), then at the top turn left along a broader track. The two routes start a long descent now, with a huge concrete water tower **[11]** and a mobile phone mast visible through the trees on your left. Soon fork right and immediately turn right to continue your descent, with garden fences on your right. Soon take a left fork, passing a playground on your left, and a little later a right fork, ignoring an old Loop fingerpost outside the wood on an old route, which somebody needs to move! Continue down to a tall pylon beside the A2022 **[Q]** – Addington Road to the right and Selsdon Park Road to the left. 🚊 *From the stop here to Addington Village tram stop.*

The route continues over the road at Ashen Vale, but you must not attempt to cross here as traffic comes very fast from both directions. Turn left for 80 metres to go behind a railing, turn right over a slip road (beware traffic coming from behind) then cross the main road at traffic lights. 🚊 *From the stop here to South, West and East Croydon stations.* Turn right on the far side, past the Church of Jesus Christ of Latter-day Saints. When the fence ends, do not follow the pavement into Ashen Vale, because the Loop now follows an ancient bridleway for 0.7 km/0.5 miles. It starts by going sharp left between the church fence and trees, then continues as a stony path between fences, crossing two quiet roads, Swallowdale and Sorrel Bank, onwards and downwards, but eventually rising to a fence and gate **[R]** into **Selsdon Wood [12]**, a nature reserve owned by the National Trust and managed by Croydon Council.

Go through the gate and up two steps, beside a tall information panel. Ignoring the path ahead turn immediately right, beside a fence, then in 10 metres left up a steep track. They give the main paths evocative names here: this one is called Addington Border, because that's what it was –

the border between the parishes of Selsdon and Addington – and at the top you pass Avis Grove and Court Wood Grove. Descending now, you reach a junction where the border route continues ahead as a short and narrow path to join a broad track, which takes you down to the far side of the wood through another gate **[S]** and fence. 🚊 *Beyond the turning circle to your left is a bus stop in Court Wood Lane, the starting point of a service to Addington Village tram stop, Hayes and Orpington. For the next 4 km/2.5 miles the Loop dodges between Greater London and Tandridge District in the county of Surrey, and a third walkers' route joins us, the Tandridge Border Path.* Turn right to climb steadily for 1.2 km/0.7 miles up an old bridleway known as **Baker Boy Lane [13]**.

You are in Surrey now, on your left is Farleigh Golf Course at first, then Puplet Wood, and higher up there is farmland on your right. Eventually, beside Old Farleigh Road, you reach and cross the entrance into Farleigh Golf Club **[T]**. The Vanguard Way goes off to the left here, but the Loop continues ahead along a bridleway, parallel with the road. In 280 metres it comes out to the road opposite Elm Farm, the first of a most delightful collection of buildings on **Farleigh Common [14]**, where a seat beside the pond makes a pleasant picnic spot. 🚌 *From a stop a little way ahead, non-TfL buses to Caterham, or to Warlingham or Selsdon for connection to central Croydon. The Harrow Inn can be reached by following a track further along the common for 0.8 km/0.5 miles, parallel with the road.*

Cross Old Farleigh Road **[U]** to follow a track to the right of Allesley Farm (the one with a weather vane). It swings left to a gate, where the route turns right down a steep, narrow and stony path – take care as there are exposed roots and barbed wire. It levels out at the head of a dry valley beside farmland, with the grand Selsdon Park Hotel occupying a prime hilltop position away to your right. Keep on to climb out of the valley through Mossyhill Shaw (shaw meaning a scrubby woodland) and cross a stile. Follow the left-hand side of a field, then with white-painted Kingswood Lodge and its brick-and-flint outbuildings over to your left, cross

another stile **[V]** on to Kingswood Lane – just a rough track at this point.

Turn left past the lodge and grazing land for 450 metres to reach the first houses in Hamsey Green, where the lane becomes a road with a pavement. Continue along it for another 500 metres to the B269 Limpsfield Road **[W]**, where Section 4 of the London Loop ends. 🚌 *From the stop on your right on the far side to Sanderstead and West Croydon.*

To continue on to Section 5, cross the road at the refuge to your right, then keep ahead past Lidl along Tithepit Shaw Lane.

5 Hamsey Green to Coulsdon South

10.2 km/6.4 miles. You can leave the route at Coulsdon Common after 6 km/3.7 miles or several other bus stops as described.

Cafés at Hamsey Green and Coulsdon. Pubs at Kenley and Coulsdon Common. Toilets at Farthing Downs. Best picnic sites: Wattenden Pond, Happy Valley, Farthing Downs.

Local authorities: Surrey County Council (Tandridge District), London Borough of Croydon.

Starting level, the route soon encounters several steep ascents, reaching the highest point of the whole London Loop, as it crosses more commons owned by the City of London. The paths and tracks are mostly in good condition but there are some long flights of steps and two stiles. You pass Kenley Aerodrome, now a base for glider-flying, then the section ends with a bracing walk along the aptly-named Happy Valley and a descent of the Farthing Downs ridge with great views.

From the Loop information panel beside the B269 Limpsfield Road at Hamsey Green **[A]**, follow the right-hand pavement of Tithepit Shaw Lane past a Lidl supermarket for 350 metres. When the road swings left, by Warlingham School, keep ahead past an information panel **[B]** along a gravel path into a vast public open space.

This is the **Sanderstead to Whyteleafe Countryside Area [1]**. Much of the land was donated by the Whitgift Foundation and management is shared between Tandridge District and Croydon Councils. The panel's map shows the names of the former farm fields here, and you stride ahead along the side of Dipsley Field.

Your immediate destination lies ahead, but the Loop must now make a great sweep northwards to avoid an old quarry and return to Croydon borough. Soon after a dew pond **[C]**, the path veers right to pass a line of oak trees, with Skylark Field now on your left. Along this stretch you pass a lichen-covered concrete pillar known as a **trig point [2]**.

Trig point is the popular term for a triangulation pillar, also known as a trigonometrical point or station, whose abbreviation gives rise to the popular term. Surprisingly, this is the only such structure that the Loop passes, but some 7,000 of them were set up in Britain from 1935 by the Ordnance Survey. Their surveyors used them to measure distances and altitudes.

When the field ends, a Loop fingerpost **[D]** turns you left along a mown grass path beside trees, with Whyteleafe

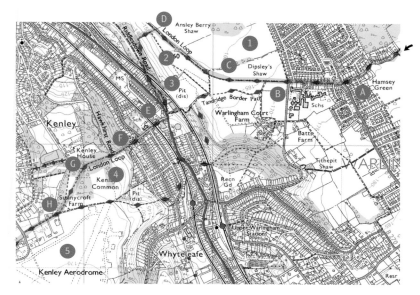

village over to your left. Go over a crossing track to drop steeply into a dry valley. Pass a fenced enclosure to enter woodland and go through a gate. You have imperceptibly entered **Riddlesdown [3]**, another of the commons owned by the City of London.

Turn left along a path then soon take a right fork down through another gate on to a stony track known as the Old Riddlesdown Road. It descends to cross the East Grinstead railway line and meet the A22 Godstone Road **[E]** on the fringe of Kenley. On your left, behind Jewsons builders' merchants, is the old quarry. This road is very busy and there's no pedestrian crossing, so take great care as you cross over then turn left for 35 metres to the corner of Old Barn Lane. *From the stop ahead to East and West Croydon. Though not a Loop link, you can reach Whyteleafe station in 0.7 km/0.5 miles by continuing along the main road to a roundabout then turn right.*

Turn right along Old Barn Lane, past Kenley Trade Park, to cross a footbridge (30 steps up and down) over the Caterham branch railway ine, then continue up New Barn Lane and across Valley Road. You may groan a little as you contemplate the climb ahead, but it will be worth the effort. You may thank the friends of Eleanor and Bob for providing a seat **[F]** here before starting up a long, zigzag flight of steps: there are 84 in all, but you must turn right at a fingerpost after the first 28. At the top you are welcomed by another City of London board, announcing your arrival on **Kenley Common [4]**.

Ignoring the field edge, go sharp right into trees to find a shady track that climbs parallel to the field to a five-ways junction with yet another City of London board – and that's the climbing done for a while! Keep ahead into woodland, surrounded by some magnificent trees, to pass one junction then continue to another at a triangular patch of grass **[G]**. Fork left, on the lesser track, soon crossing another track to reach a large field at a marooned gate. Go diagonally across, heading for a similar gate – these gates must surely be a relic from the time when they marked the line of an old right of way across farmland.

Pass a fingerpost, then a great oak with a bench at its foot, to cut across a woodland corner and join a track, where turn right past a City of London board to a gate **[H]**. *The Loop continues ahead, but it's worth a 100-metre detour through a small gate on your left to see* **Kenley Aerodrome [5]**.

Kenley Aerodrome is the last of London's Battle of Britain fighter stations to survive in its World War II form. To your left is the grass bank of a blast bay where Spitfires from one of Kenley's three squadrons sheltered. Way across the field, the officers' mess and one of the operations huts still stand. Today, Kenley is only a glider training school, and it's difficult to relate this peaceful scene with the crunch of Luftwaffe bombs and the roar of Merlin engines.

Go straight ahead along unmade Golf Road (the aerodrome was constructed on a golf course) to reach Hayes Lane **[I]**. Turn right along the lane, but take care as there is no pavement. *There is a possibility that the route may be diverted here in the near future – watch out for diversion signs. Another interesting leftward diversion here, to recently restored Wattenden Pond, which has*

seats and a picnic table and some attractive flint cottages nearby.

In 130 metres, just before the first house on the left, go left on a footpath. At a path junction, turn right and very soon emerge on to the open grass of **Betts Mead Recreation Ground [6]**, where you go diagonally left, across the corner, with some houses away to your right. Turn left across a slight dip and through a gap into another field, then left again along its edge. Towards the end of this field, veer slightly right on a worn path to a fingerpost and go down a few steps on to Old Lodge Lane **[J]**, but take great care as you step directly into the path of oncoming traffic. *Just 100 metres to your left is the Wattenden Arms pub, a favourite with airmen from Kenley in wartime, of which it has much memorabilia; on the way, note the pretty Thatched Cottage, which was once another pub, the Pig & Whistle.*

Cross the lane on to the drive of The Haven, but immediately cross a stile on your left and follow the left-hand side of the field. Bear slightly right to go through a gate behind a tall bush and continue beside another field, aiming for a white dome ahead and now with Kenley Aerodrome to your left. Across another stile, the dome turns out to be an observatory **[7]**, and hiding behind it a baby one, surely the world's tiniest observatory! They belong to the Croydon Astronomical Society.

Join the grit drive of Cornwall Farm through a gate and in 50 metres, at a meeting of ways **[K]** beside the gate of Briar Cottage, turn right to drop down between concrete bollards on an old sunken track known as Waterhouse Lane. It descends steeply then levels out between fences to reach Caterham Drive **[L]** on the edge of Old Coulsdon. Cross straight over and keep ahead up Rydons Lane, which has pavements at first, but they run out halfway and you must continue with care up a 325-metre stretch with no footway, especially where it becomes quite dark under trees near the top. Cross busier Stites Hill Road **[M]** and a horseride to follow the broad track ahead on **Coulsdon Common [8]**, another City of London area and the highest point of the whole London Loop at 177 metres/580 feet, to emerge at and cross the B2030 Coulsdon Road. *From the stop on this side to Caterham; from the far side to Purley Oaks and East Croydon, also (not Sundays) to Coulsdon South.*

On your right, dwarfing the adjacent bus stop, there's an enormous antique sign for the Fox pub **[9],** which you will soon pass as you continue along a mown path through grass to the right of Fox Lane to another City of London board, though of a different shape. Go under a height limiter **[N]** to follow a tarmac track beside a car park and past a barrier, then along the right-hand side of a vast field. At its end, on a rougher surface, continue down through trees into aptly named **Happy Valley [10]**, a glorious expanse of grass downland, where you are indeed on the northern fringe of the North Downs, as patches of chalk reveal as you continue down on springy turf past some seats.

Through a belt of trees there's an odd wooden contraption **[O]**: is it a double-decker seat or a narrow picnic table at which you sit with your back to the view? This would be a shame as it must be one of the finest views in all of London. Descend left beside trees, across the floor of this dry valley,

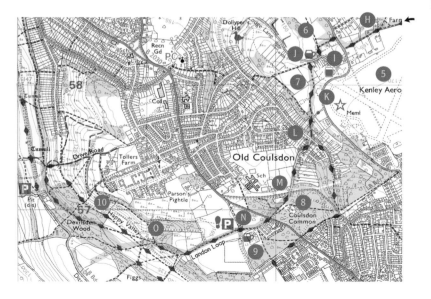

Swinging down from Coulsdon Common into Happy Valley, the Loop treats you to some of the best chalk downland near London.

past one fingerpost, then continue up to another, where you turn right on a grassy path beside more trees. It leads unerringly into **Devilsden Wood [11]**, where you join one of the Happy Valley Nature Trails to climb steadily for 550 metres into more grassland at **Farthing Downs [12]**, the last bit of land owned by the City of London in this part of the Loop.

Just a little further up, to your left, cross Ditches Lane **[P]** into a car park *(toilets to your left, and there may be an ice-cream van)* and turn right along the path on its far side. To avoid putting signs into this sensitive landscape, the Loop formally keeps to the road, but the sensible thing is to walk along the grass sward, with parts of Coulsdon on either side. The cattle are sometimes put out to graze here – they are of a docile breed, but best keep your distance. A tall square tower over to your left was part of Cane Hill Asylum, most of which is now residential. You pass a neat circle of wooden seats beside a panoply of information panels, and further on, approaching a copse, a stone plinth to your right is surmounted by a topograph.

The copse turns out to be The Folly, where in 1783 a local landowner planted seven beech trees, of which just one remains, though new ones have been planted to restore the number. An antique fingerpost **[Q]** here tells you that Coulsdon lies to the right, but that's the old village, so the Loop continues ahead in the Purley direction, with modern Coulsdon soon appearing ahead. Away to your left now is the belfry atop St Andrew's Church, and to your right the scar of an old chalk quarry and another distant view of those transmitters.

A row of neat, brick-tiled houses appears ahead, and you leave the downs through a gate **[R]**. Go left across Downs Road then continue down its pavement to reach the busy B276 Marlpit Road. Ignore the Loop signs opposite – there's no need to cross over *(unless you want to visit the café in Coulsdon Memorial Ground, whose entrance lies 30 metres to your right)*. Turn left then very soon left again into Reddown Road. Cross over at Hadleigh Grove and continue on the far side for 60 metres, where turn right down steps on to a tarmac path leading to Coulsdon South station **[S]** ⇌ where Section 5 of the Loop ends. Just a few more steps though:

25 to Platfom 2 for Gatwick Airport and Brighton, and another 21 up and down to Platform 1 for East Croydon, Clapham Junction and central London. *There are pubs and cafés in Coulsdon town centre, just a little way along Section 6.*

To continue on to Section 6, pass through the ticket office then turn right down the forecourt, where are situated the station's bus stops. 🚌 *From the stop on this side to Redhill; far side to West Croydon and Wallington.*

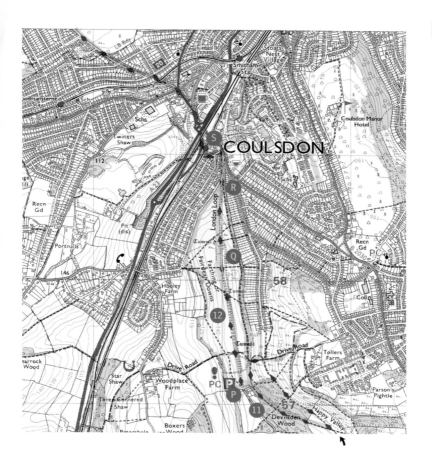

6 Coulsdon South to Banstead Downs

7.6 km/4.7 miles plus link to Banstead station 0.5 km/0.3 miles. You can leave the route at The Oaks Park after 4.3 km/2.7 miles. On Sundays, as there is no public transport at Banstead station, you would have to walk to Banstead village for a bus, adding 1 km/0.6 miles, or you can catch a bus from Sutton Lane 1.3 km/0.8 miles before the finish.

Cafés in Coulsdon town centre and Oaks Park. Refreshment kiosk at Mayfield Lavender Fields (summer only). Pub at Clock House Village. Toilets at Coulsdon South station and Oaks Park. Best picnic opportunity: Oaks Park.

Local authorities: London Boroughs of Croydon and Sutton, Surrey County Council (Reigate & Banstead District).

This section of the Loop starts with a steady ascent through residential parts of Coulsdon then levels out in high, open country, where five stiles are encountered, to go through lavender fields and Oaks Park. Finally a long, straight and level bridleway leads past High Down prison to Banstead Downs Golf Course.

Leaving Coulsdon South Station's main exit **[A]** on Platform 1, go across the forecourt and down steps to use a light-controlled crossing over the A237 Brighton Road. Turn right on the far side to go under a railway bridge and then the Coulsdon Bypass flyover to a roundabout. Pass the entrance to Cane Hill Park and keep ahead to a set of traffic lights, where the road divides: Brighton Road goes ahead into Coulsdon's town centre but the Loop forks left along Lion Green Road. Pass a car park to more traffic lights and cross Chipstead Valley Road **[B]** to keep ahead up Woodman Road. Cross to the right-hand side, then a short way up just around a bend, immediately after house number 26, go right up a driveway and bear left along a path and through a barrier. Cross the Tattenham Corner branch railway to reach Woodmansterne Road, cross it and turn left, then soon bear right at a junction, still in Woodmansterne Road.

The Loop now climbs ahead for 0.8 km/0.5 miles, crossing Bramley Avenue **[C]**. Where the pavement runs out, you enter the London Borough of Sutton to continue along a grass verge, and the road changes its name to Grove Lane. At the top, clustered around a green with a majestic oak tree, is **Clock House village [1]**. *The Jack & Jill pub and a food shop lie to the left.* 🚌 *From the stop on the green to Wallington and Mitcham Eastfields; from the stop further left to Coulsdon South.*

Keep ahead along a tarmac footway past the pub for 90 metres, then take an uneven, stony path between high hedges, though this is still part of Grove Lane, parallel with the road at first.

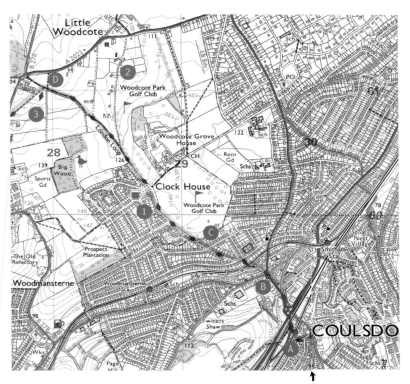

Look out on the left for an iron plate of 1898, marking the boundary of the now-departed Carshalton District. The clacking sounds to your right will be from Woodcote Park Golf Course. The road turns away as you keep on through abandoned iron gates, then fork left beside a field, with the **Little Woodcote Estate [2]** away to your right.

The path leads to a bend in a farm track, on which you keep ahead until it swings left through a gate, but you go between steel posts on your right to follow a narrow path. Keep ahead at a crossing track, then in 35 metres turn left, leaving Grove Lane to go through squeeze-posts **[D]**, which may be hidden in shrubbery, into **Carshalton Road Pastures [3]**. A worn path leads ahead through the grass, with some

sheds down to your right, and up a shallow bank, then veers slightly right to cross a slight dip in a hedgerow on its way to the far corner. Go through more squeeze-posts and carefully step out on to the B278 Carshalton Road, having checked both ways for approaching traffic. Turn left along it – there is a narrow verge, but you may have to step aside to let vehicles pass. In 170 metres at some houses and just before '30' speed signs **[E]**, cross over to house 'Thirty Three' then go sharp right over a stile into a field. Walk beside the left-hand hedge, and when it turns away bear right across the field, heading for the tallest tree.

Cross two stiles to enter **Mayfield Lavender Fields [4]** and keep ahead along its broad, central track, enjoying

Swathes of fragrant lavender at Mayfield.

the heady scent, with swathes of the fragrant plant stretching almost as far as you can see. Our path is a right of way, but you must not stray into the lavender on either side. Cross a stile **[F]** on the far side, but do not cross the road at this point; instead turn right for 90 metres beside the field to another stile then go left over a light-controlled crossing. *In lavender season (late June to early September) you may*

wish to keep ahead for 100 metres to take advantage of the pop-up café, shop and toilets at the lavender centre, or even pay the entry fee and wander at will among the plants.  *To Purley and West Croydon from the stop in Carshalton Road, just past the Mayfields entrance.*

Across the road, keep ahead through a black gate into **Oaks Park [5]** and immediately turn left along a stony path through trees, with picnic tables to your right. Veering right, the path reaches the junction of broad tarmac drives, with the park café and toilets nearby. Turn left between low fences, watching out for traffic, as this is the park's main entrance.

The house of Oaks Park was demolished in 1860, but the Derby family, who took over the estate in the 1700s, gave it a colourful reputation as a hunting and racing centre, keeping staghounds and spreading the fame of Oaks Park far and wide with extravagant fêtes and parties. One race, The Oaks, took its name from the estate, and legend tells of the 12th Earl tossing a coin with Sir Charles Bunbury to decide the name for another new flat race. Commented David Sharp, "'The Derby' won, and it's difficult to imagine those colourful crowds flocking to Epsom Downs to watch a race called 'The Bunbury'!"

In a few metres, at a Loop fingerpost and information panel, turn right along a broad tarmac path through ornamental gardens with an array of seats. The path narrows and bends left into shrubbery, still on tarmac. When that ends at a wooden barrier, bear right on an earth path, then immediately right again, then left among trees to keep near the parallel road on your left. At a short fence, go down a few steps to continue in the same direction beside a higher fence, which you follow round to the left at a corner. Back near the road **[G]**, turn right on a rough lane, known as Fairlawn Road, and follow it for 200 metres to the first house on the left (Rivendell). Turn left up an ancient green way called Freedown Lane, an uneven, rutted, stony and shrub-lined bridleway, which leads you into the Reigate & Banstead District of Surrey. You follow it for 1.7 km/1.1 miles, soon passing stables and a large barn, and climbing past a junction. Halfway along, behind a fence and wall on your right, you may glimpse the much higher walls of **High Down prison [6]**.

At Casa Miel ('honey house' in Spanish), the lane continues on rough tarmac to reach B2218 Sutton Lane **[H]**. 🚌 *From the stop to your left to Belmont, Sutton and Mitcham Junction.* Cross over and take the track ahead on to **Banstead Downs [7]**, with a fine stretch of broom and birch heathland to your right. Ignoring side turnings, drop down to a junction of waymarked trails, then keep ahead across the branch railway line to Epsom Downs **[I]**. Take the left fork and follow the main track, still ignoring side turnings. You soon reach Banstead Downs Golf Course and keep ahead on a worn path, with first a tee to your left, then a green to your right. *Don't forget to let golfers finish their stroke before going past!*

The path continues between trees to reach a waymark post beside a fairway, where you continue on a worn grass track, now with a green to your left and a group of tees to your right. At the furthest tee, follow a track around to the right to reach the very busy A217, another Brighton Road **[J]**. *As there are no trains or buses on Sundays from Banstead Station, you may need to follow the link to the bus stop in Banstead town centre, which starts here.*

Link with Banstead town centre and bus stop (0.9 km/0.6 miles). Turn left along the roadside footway (also a cycle track) to cross a concrete-walled railway bridge and pass a driveway, then immediately fork left along a path through dense bushes. At the end, cross carefully over A2022 Winkworth Road **[K]** by a roundabout and follow the footway ahead beside B2219 Bolters Lane, which climbs for 0.7 km/0.5 miles. At the top, go over the light-controlled crossing **[L]** and turn left at another roundabout into Banstead High Street. Buses go from the stop outside Marks & Spencer to Sutton, Coulsdon, Purley Oaks and West Croydon. There are several cafés along the High Street and toilets behind NatWest Bank, also the Woolpack pub at the far end of the High Street.

Returning from Banstead town centre, go to Zizzi restaurant by the roundabout and cross at the lights to your right **[L]**, then turn right down the far side of Bolters Lane for 0.7 km/0.5 miles. At the bottom, cross Winkworth Road **[K]** at the refuge then follow the path ahead into woodland. At A217 Brighton Road, turn right over the concrete-walled railway bridge to the golf club access **[J]**, where you rejoin the Loop.

You must now cross the two carriageways of the A217 with extreme care via the central reservation, in company with golfers who also have to use this crossing between the two parts of their course. At the access drive into the western part, immediately turn right on a narrow and possibly overgrown path to reach a waymark post beside the golf course. Keep ahead diagonally

across the fairway, checking both ways for flying golf balls, to come beside a line of trees, with a tee to your left and bunkers to your right. Head for a waymark post indicating where you go back into more dense scrub along a narrow path. In 30 metres it comes to a Loop fingerpost **[M]**, at which unremarkable spot, the route planners decided to end Section 6 – possibly because it's the nearest point to Banstead Station, for which the link starts here.

To continue on to Section 7, just keep ahead.

Link to Banstead Station (0.5 km/0.3 miles, no Sunday trains). Turn left at the Loop fingerpost along an equally narrow path – beware overhanging branches. Shortly keep ahead at a junction of golfers tracks, then take a right fork to a fairway. Cross it in the same direction, towards trees along a slightly sunken route with a green to your left. On the far side, turn left up the right-hand side of the green to find a path into the trees, which leads to Banstead Road. Cross over and turn left on the far pavement, which leads around the bend to Banstead Station **[N]** 🚆 (no toilets).

7 Banstead Downs to Ewell

5.5 km/3.5 miles, plus links from Banstead station (0.5 km/0.3 miles) and to Ewell West station (0.5 km/0.3 miles). You can leave the route at Cheam Road after 2.8 km/1.8 miles or Ewell East after 4.7 km/2.9 miles. On Sundays, as there is no public transport at Banstead station, you may have to go by bus to Banstead village, adding 1.4 km/0.9 miles (see Section 6 for the link route description), or you can take a bus to start at Sutton Lane near the end of Section 6, adding 1.3 km/0.8 miles.

Cafés and toilets at Nonsuch Park (0.6 km/0.4 miles off route) and Ewell. Pubs at Ewell. Best picnic opportunities: Nonsuch Park, Bourne Hall Park.

Local authorities: Surrey County Council (Reigate & Banstead and Epsom & Ewell Districts), London Borough of Sutton.

Starting high up on Banstead Downs Golf Course the Loop starts a long descent back to the Thames valley. There's a stretch along residential roads in Belmont, leading to Warren Farm and Nonsuch Park, which has traces of one of Henry VIII's palaces. The section finishes in the gardens of Bourne Hall Park in Ewell.

Loop link from Banstead station

(0.5 km/0.3 miles, no Sunday service). From the station exit **[A]** turn left along the pavement and around the bend for 140 metres, until opposite Cuddington Park Close. Cross over to a Loop fingerpost and follow a path into trees, soon taking a right fork to emerge by a green on **Banstead Downs Golf Course [1]**. Go half left around the edge of the green, first allowing golfers to finish their stroke before proceeding. Follow a slightly sunken route to the right of a fairway, heading for a waymark post beside trees. Keep ahead into the trees, soon reaching a track junction and taking a possibly overgrown path heading into dense scrub (not the track to its left), which leads to a Loop fingerpost **[B]**, where you turn left to rejoin the Loop.

From the Loop fingerpost **[B]**, keep ahead on the narrow path in woodland to emerge briefly at a group of tees with a rustic seat. Continue on the path through more woodland, soon emerging beside some well spaced trees with a fairway to your right. Keep on, now with a wildflower meadow on your left, and follow a line of birch trees towards houses – but beware golfers teeing off in your direction. On reaching the tees, head for another wooden seat **[C]** then bear right along a path between bushes, which leads to houses in Sandy Lane in the Belmont district of Sutton borough.

Follow the left-hand pavement beside Sandy Lane – a popular practice course for driving schools. In 600 metres you reach a pair of little white gates **[D]** marking the entrance to Cuddington Way. Turn left here, walking along the grass verge, then take the first right, Cheyham Way, with more white gates, using the left-hand pavement to reach the busier Northey Avenue **[E]**, where you turn left for another 600 metres. There are Loop signs opposite, but do not cross here because there's a blind bend to your right. There is no pedestrian crossing along this road, but turn left along the left-hand pavement to a sign proclaiming your entry into Epsom & Ewell District in Surrey, and soon after it cross over where visibility is better to continue along the far pavement.

On reaching a big roundabout by the modern **St Paul's Church [2]**, turn sharp right into Nonsuch Walk, a side road beside A232 Cheam Road. Go over grass a short way to pick up a tarmac footway between the two roads and follow it for 250 metres to a bus shelter **[F]**. 🚌 *From this stop to Ewell East and Epsom; from the the far side to Cheam, Sutton, Morden and Colliers Wood.* Cross Cheam Road and continue along Bramley Avenue, the turning opposite. At the bottom, cross Holmwood Road and head along a drive that leads you under the London to Portsmouth railway line, and on into **Warren Farm [3]**.

Keep ahead on a track along the right-hand side of a large field, coming

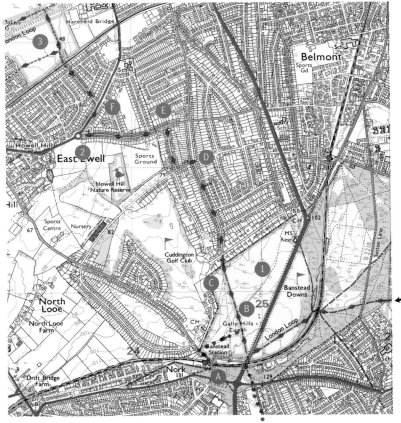

shortly to a Loop fingerpost **[G]**, telling you that this is where the link to Ewell East Station starts.

Link with Ewell East Station

(1.2 km/0.7 miles, for trains to Clapham Junction, London Victoria and Epsom). Turn left along a track that leads to the far left end of the field, then after two benches bear left through a gate to reach houses in Seymour Avenue. Keep straight ahead along it for 0.8 km/½ mile, crossing Castlemaine Avenue and past Parr Avenue, where it changes name to Nonsuch Court Avenue. At the A232 Cheam Road, cross at the lights then turn left and shortly right to the station **[H]**. **Returning from the station**, go through the car park to Cheam Road and turn left to cross at the lights. Walk up Nonsuch Court Avenue and pass Parr Avenue, where it becomes Seymour Avenue, then cross Castlemaine Avenue and continue to a gate into Warren Farm. Bear left then immediately fork right and cross the field to a Loop fingerpost **[G]**. Turn left to rejoin the route.

The Loop continues ahead into a belt of trees, where you cross a pair of parallel concrete tracks and keep on to another Loop fingerpost **[I]** beside a tarmac drive in **Nonsuch Park [4]**, once a royal hunting ground. *Café and toilets at Nonsuch Mansion [5], 0.6 km/0.4 miles to your right here.* Turn left along the drive, which is also a cycle route, for 0.6 km/0.4 miles to reach Castlemaine Lodge **[J]**.

The site of **Nonsuch Palace [6]** was excavated in 1959. Henry VIII seems to have devoted his last years to the creation of Nonsuch – the name was Henry's boast that it would have no equal – but he never saw it finished and Elizabeth I made far more use of it. But in true Henry VIII style, he had the village of Cuddington destroyed to make way for his palace – the excavations revealed the outline of Cuddington church beneath the palace courtyards, a little further along the diversion.

Back at Castlemaine Lodge, keep ahead up a track to pass a concrete pillar bearing the number 2, then almost immediately fork right on a simple earth path through woodland. It passes pillars 3 and 4, then at a cross-tracks with pillar number 5 turn right and soon find yourself walking beside a roughly rectangular platform with corner bastions, all held together by brick walls: though heavily overgrown now, this was the site of the **banqueting hall [7]** of Nonsuch Palace.

Keep on to the corner of a grassy field then turn left along its edge to the next corner, where steps lead down to the very busy dual carriageway A24 Ewell Bypass **[K]**. There is no light-controlled crossing to help you over, but dropped kerbs to your left indicate where pedestrians are expected to cross with extreme care via the central reservation.

On the far side, keep ahead through a gap in a hedge to go half right over a side road and down more steps to a tarmac footpath known as Vicarage

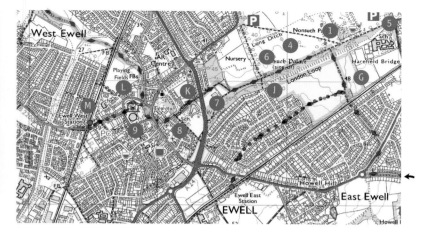

Lane. It leads between fences, with Ewell Castle School on your left and the mansard roofs of residential Holman Court on your right, to **Church Street [8]** in Ewell, where several notable buildings vie for your attention (see page 74).

At its end is the High Street, where the Loop turns right. *The Star pub, cafés and food shops are to your left here.* At pedestrian traffic lights, cross over to pass through the white archway known as Dog Gate (look up to its top!) into **Bourne Hall Park [9]**, which closes half an hour before dusk. 🚌 *There are three bus stops here: the first for an hourly bus to Chessington South, the second for Stoneleigh Park and Worcester Park, and the third (opposite) for Epsom (non-TfL).*

Pass the white lodge then bear right on a broad tarmac path beside the lake. To your left, up a grassy slope, is Bourne Hall, which has a café and toilets and plenty of seats scattered around. You pass under a magnificent deodar (a type of cedar) and on the far side of

the lawn is a golden-rain tree, which can be very colourful when its yellow flowers and pink fruit are out. At the end of the lake are a Loop fingerpost **[L]** and information panel, where Section 7 of the Loop ends.

To continue on to Section 8, keep ahead past the Loop fingerpost. The Spring Tavern is just 150 metres away along Section 8.

Link to Ewell West Station
(0.5 km/0.3 miles, for trains to Wimbledon, Clapham Junction, Vauxhall, London Waterloo, Epsom and Dorking). Turn left at the Loop fingerpost, soon forking right on a path that bends left to follow the walled edge of the park. At a T-junction, turn right to exit through a gate in the wall, then turn left to a three-way road junction. Cross to the right-hand pavement then turn left for 200 metres along the B2200 Chessington Road to find Ewell West station **[M]** 🚆 on your right.

Banstead Downs to Ewell

8 Ewell to Kingston Bridge

11.6 km/7.2 miles, plus links from Ewell West station (0.5 km/0,3 miles) and to Kingston station (0.6 km/0.4 miles). You can leave the route at Malden Manor after 6.6 km/4.1 miles, Berrylands after 8.8 km/5.5 miles or several bus stops as described.

Cafés at Bourne Hall Park, Ewell Court Park, Malden Manor, Berrylands, Kingston. Pubs at New Malden, Berrylands, Kingston. Toilets at Bourne Hall Park, Ewell Court Park. Best picnic opportunities: Ewell Court Park, Berrylands.

Local authorities: Surrey County Council (Epsom & Ewell District), Royal Borough of Kingston-upon-Thames.

Most of the route is on level, sometimes rough or muddy, ground closely following the Hogsmill River to its confluence with the Thames at Kingston. But you have to divert away from it twice where the riverside is not accessible to the public: first to climb through residential roads in Old Malden, and again approaching Kingston, where there are many historical associations, to finish beside the ancient bridge over the Thames.

Link from Ewell West Station

(0.4 km/0.3 miles). From the station exit **[A]**, go ahead between houses to Chessington Road and turn left to the three-way junction with Spring Street. Cross at the lights and follow the brick wall to a gate into Bourne Hall Park*. Turn left along the path that leads to the Loop fingerpost **[B]** by the lake, then turn left to rejoin the route.

*Opening times for the park vary between about 8 and 9 am, so if the gate is closed you should go left across grass and follow the road round to the right, past a health centre, to rejoin the Loop where it comes out of the next park gate and turns right to traffic lights.

Section 8 of the Loop starts at the Loop fingerpost **[B]** beside the lake in Bourne Hall Park. Walking on

beyond the lake, you pass an old metal waterwheel, now waterless under a stone arch. Leave the park into Chessington Road. Traffic comes fast around the bend from the right, so keep close to the right-hand side as you turn right to traffic lights, beside a pond, and with the Spring Tavern ahead across Kingston Road. Cross at the lights and keep ahead on a tarmac path into trees, with a millstream over to your left. This is the start of the long and narrow Hogsmill Local Nature Reserve, and you will be walking beside either the **Hogsmill River**

[1] or one of its many millstreams, or one of the long and narrow parallel meadows, for the next 4 km/2.5 miles.

Just as you left the Thames by following the waters of the Darent and Cray from Crossness, so you return to it beside the Hogsmill, another of London's little known rivers. It rises from the lake in Bourne Hall Park and several other ponds and springs nearby then flows for 9.9 km/6 miles to Kingston. Like the Cray, the Hogsmill has its own trail, the Hogsmill Walk, and the Loop has presumed to latch on for its whole length.

Soon you come alongside white, weatherboarded **Upper Mill [2]** and the Loop turns left in front of it to cross the millstream. Turn right on the far side, still on tarmac but now with the stream on your right and the river over to your left. When the tarmac path swings left, bear right on a stony path beneath trees, which crosses a footbridge that seems to be egging you on to walk the plank ahead, where river and millstream come together, but best take the safer option of another footbridge to your left, which crosses a little tributary stream. The path continues close to the river now, crossing one narrow leat, then another beside the remains of an old mill.

Shortly the Loop takes advantage of an ingenious device, a raised wooden causeway **[C]** above the river, and together they squeeze under an embankment carrying the railway that you may have just used to reach Ewell West. Be sure to duck under a

low pipe at the far end! Turn right then left over grass, with the river and the remnants of another old mill to your left. The grass leads on to a riverside track, which may be muddy, and a meadow, thought to be where William Holman Hunt painted his 'The Hireling Shepherd' in 1851. At an information panel, resist the temptation to skip across stepping stones in the river – they may be slippery. Instead, keep ahead among trees to pass a fenced enclosure containing the **Ewell Storm Tanks [3]**, which are intended to prevent overflow water from flooding the meadows after heavy rain.

Your route crosses the next footbridge, as indicated by a Loop fingerpost. *But before doing that, you may wish to make a short rightward diversion into* **Ewell Court Park [4]** *which has picnic tables, an old packhorse bridge, a large duckpond and Ewell Court itself, a handsome red-brick mansion of 1879, now a library and function venue. There is a café with toilets (closed Mondays) in the nursery garden behind the mansion.*

After crossing the river, turn right so that it is on your right again, while an athletics arena behind a fence to your left in King George's Field is the home of Epsom & Ewell Harriers. At a playground, another footbridge takes you back over, and you turn left on a broad grit track, with the river now to your left and a meadow to your right. In these watermeadows, with their graceful stands of trees, you catch an occasional glimpse of rooftops. Watch out for cyclists now as most of the tracks are used by them.

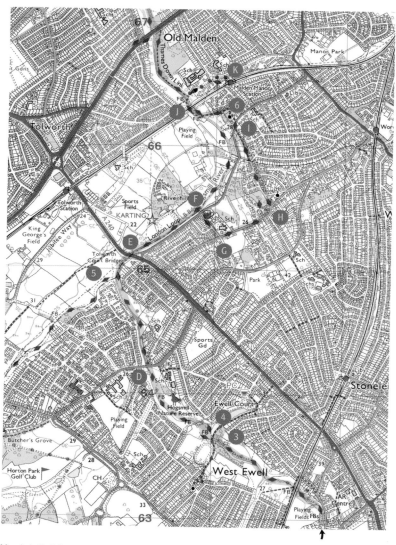

You briefly join a tarmac path, which comes across the river then starts away rightwards, but you keep ahead on a dirt track to stay beside the river, and soon cross the B284 Ruxley Lane **[D]** at pedestrian lights. 🚌 *From the stop up to your left to Tolworth and Kingston, and there's a Co-op food store further up.* Continue past a barrier along a

tarmac path with the river to your left and houses to your right. At another barrier, the path surface changes to grit and you pass (but do not cross) a footbridge by a grand old weeping willow, then a playground, to a junction beside another footbridge. You should ignore this one too, but notice the white 'through-arch' bridge beyond, under which the **Bonesgate Stream [5]** flows to join the Hogsmill making it noticeably wider from here on. The Bonesgate brings with it the 24-km/15-mile Thames Down Link, which as its name suggests links the Thames at Kingston with the North Downs. The three trails march together for the next 7 km/4 miles into Kingston, with their separate logos adorning the waymark posts. Continue along the right bank to the A240 Kingston Road at Tolworth Court Bridge **[E]**.

The route continues opposite, but the road is much too busy to cross here, so you should turn right to cross at the traffic lights. 🚌 *From the stop on this side to Tolworth and Kingston; from the far side to Epsom.* Turn left on the far side, crossing the two spurs of Worcester Park Road and watching out for traffic coming from the left at the second spur as there's no pedestrian crossing there. Keep ahead, back across the bridge, looking over the parapet to see the river cascading down lines of boulders. On the far side, turn right through a sad, neglected and rather overgrown iron gateway that was only installed in 1973 by nearby Surbiton Town Sports Club in memory of a long-serving secretary. Pass the barrier inside to follow a narrow, stony path, with the river to your right, and soon an information panel above a go-kart track. On reaching a lane called Riverhill, turn right over the river on a bridge **[F]** with curious little viewing recesses.

There is as yet no path that continues beside the river here, and the long, parallel lane is narrow with no pavement or verge, so the Loop has

to make a diversion of 1.5 km/1 mile which is a shame, as we miss the likely location in the Hogsmill where in 1852 Sir John Millais painted his most famous work, 'Ophelia', singing as she drowns. And so, with a sigh, cross the B284 Old Malden Lane to the Toby Carvery pub (formerly the Hogsmill Tavern) and keep ahead up the left-hand pavement of Cromwell Road to a crossroads **[G]**.

Turn left along Grafton Road to pass Linden Bridge School, then climb for 400 metres to the junction at the top with Delta Road. Bear left along The Avenue to reach a little island of trees **[H]**, where you fork left to follow Royal Avenue, a thoroughfare with a split personality: starting as a short cul-de-sac, it continues briefly as a tarmac path, then an unmade road, and finally a broad tarmac road. Cross over to continue along the right-hand pavement to a T-junction **[I]**, with Highdown to the right and Barrow Hill dropping steeply to the left. Cross over to keep ahead past a barrier, entering the London Borough of Kingston along a grit path between a fence and woodland for 300 metres. It drops to meet that perilous B284 again, which has now acquired a new name, Church Road, and thankfully a pavement, to which you should cross and turn right. Shortly turn left on an unmade road to pass the red-brick church of **St John the Baptist, Malden [6]**.

The church is now an odd, patchwork mixture. You can see medieval flintwork in the chancel, but nave and tower are simple brick from the early 17th century. Not to be left out, the Victorians added their own nave and chancel, requiring the church to be reconsecrated. Malden derives from the Saxon *mael-dun*, a cross on a hill, and here stands the little church on its hill above the Hogsmill, probably the religious site that gave its name to Old Malden.

Past the churchyard, go through the gate of Manor Farm Cottages and follow the stony track as it drops leftwards beside a fence, with trees to your left, back to the Hogsmill. Don't cross the footbridge but go slightly right along a narrow path, which leads under a remarkably high concrete bridge with peekaboo arches, carrying the branch railway line to Chessington South. Continue to a junction **[J]** with a tarmac track, where the link with Malden Manor Station starts.

Link with Malden Manor Station (380 metres). Turn right up the broad tarmac shared-use track (keep right) then go ahead along Sheephouse Way between blocks of flats. At the end, by a tree-covered roundabout (*café, food shop*) turn right into Manor Drive North and cross at the refuge to the station **[K]** ⇌ (40 steps up, no toilets). **Returning from the station**, turn left beside the forecourt to Manor Drive North, cross at the refuge then turn right. Bear left at the roundabout then turn left along Sheephouse Way. At the end, keep ahead down the shared-use tarmac track (keep left) to a junction **[J]** at the foot, where you should turn right to rejoin the Loop.

Immediately beyond the tarmac track, you are faced with a choice of path. The Loop takes the left fork, briefly rejoining the river but soon coming out to the aptly named Long Meadows, four of them, linked by paths through shrubbery. Finally you pass an information panel for the Hogsmill Valley Walk, adding a fourth partner to this well-used riverside conduit, and follow a broad grass track to the monstrous A3 Malden Way **[L]**, part of the Kingston Bypass. It has four lanes, two of which form the main dual carriageway, plus a parallel service road on either side. The Loop continues opposite, but to cross here would be madness as there's no pedestrian facility, so the Loop must make a 400-metre diversion. Turn left to reach a bus stop **[M]** (🚌 *for Tolworth, Surbiton and Kingston*) beside a food shop and cross the side road (traffic goes both ways here) to go through the subway.

On the far side, turn right and double back towards the river (🚌 *Malden Manor, New Malden, Barnes and Putney Bridge*) past an apartment block, then where it ends turn left through a gap. Take the right fork back to the river, where a concrete structure ushers the Tolworth Stream into the Hogsmill. You now follow a lovely riverside stretch called Elmbridge Meadows for 1 km/0.6 miles, getting ever lovelier as you leave the A3 behind, with a nature reserve on the far bank. *In 100 metres, a footbridge [N] and path to your right (turn left at the end) lead in 400 metres to Woodies Free House in New Malden, an idiosyncratic pub in a sports pavilion.* Continue by the river, soon with the sports ground of Kings College London

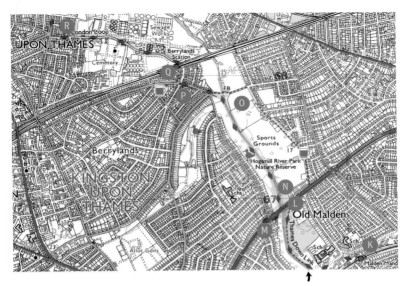

beyond the far bank, and ignoring all attempts to lead you leftwards.

Eventually you cross a footbridge **[O]** over the Surbiton Stream to a grass area with a picnic table and keep ahead to a broad tarmac shared-use track, with the houses of Berrylands over to your left. The riverside path ahead soon meets an impenetrable barrier in the shape of a railway embankment, so the Loop and its companions must now leave the riverside again to follow pavements and paths into Kingston – though we shall be reunited with the Hogsmill there.

Turn left along the tarmac track (keep right) to a roundabout and go ahead past the roundabout to follow the right-hand pavement of a road called Surbiton Hill Park. *Far side to Surbiton; this side further on to Tolworth and Kingston.* Keep on to another roundabout **[P]** beside the Berrylands pub and turn right down Chiltern Drive *(café, food shop)* to

Berrylands Station [Q] on the main line from Waterloo to Woking and the south west *(50 steps up to the platforms, no toilets).* Go past the station sign on a tarmac shared-use track (keep left) through a tunnel under the railway to join Lower Marsh Lane. This once green way must have been an attractive route in the past, but nowadays it treats you to a cemetery, a sewage works and light industry, becoming residential later.

In 0.8 km/0.5 miles you reach a busy road junction **[R]** and turn right along the right-hand side of Villiers Road, passing a roundabout and with the Duke of Buckingham pub opposite *From both stops nearby to Kingston.* Cross several side roads to reach Athelstan Recreation Ground, then cross the Hogsmill again to Dawson Road. Go over the zebra crossing and continue on the far side past the blue mesh fence **[S]** of Kingston Town Children's Centre, where you turn left along the tarmac Swan Path. This leads to a lane beside an entrance into Kingston University, back by the Hogsmill. Cross a bridge **[T]** over the river and turn right along Three Bridges Path. Cross a second channel on the first of those bridges then turn right, beside a wire mesh fence, to follow a more modest riverside path – and it becomes apparent that the Hogsmill's water has been joined by unsavoury supplements.

At a blue girder bridge, turn left to join Springfield Road briefly, go past a barrier then turn sharp right along Denmark Road. Beyond an apartment block and its car park, take a path to your right, back to the river. Keep ahead at a junction beside the Hogsmill Community Garden to emerge at the dual carriageway A240 Penrhyn Road **[U]** in the heart of Kingston. Cross over at the two-stage controlled pedestrian lights ahead, then turn right along the pavement as it swings left past College Roundabout to another set of lights. Cross again and walk ahead into St James's Road. Almost immediately, just before it crosses the Hogsmill, turn left on a riverside path, which goes through and even under the Guildhall Complex. The semi-circular building at the end, on the far bank, is the Guildhall itself, surmounted by an extraordinary octagonal turret with a small dome, then on top of all that a weathervane. The path leads to the High Street, where you go over a zebra crossing.

But before doing so, turn right over the Hogsmill to see the venerable **Coronation Stone [7]**, protected by a blue fence linking seven stone columns. Further along to the right is Kingston's bustling Market Place.

"The Coronation Stone has moved around quite a bit, and now rests in the Guildhall car park, very convenient for the Mayor's Rolls, and whatever conveyances were used by the Saxon kings. By tradition, seven of them, starting in the year 900 with Edward the Elder, were crowned on this cold block of stone. Further along to the right here is the market place, the bustling heart of Kingston with its stalls overlooked by a cheerfully Italianate market hall of 1840, fronted by a gaudily gilded statue of Queen Anne, rescued from an earlier town hall." *David Sharp*

Across the High Street, turn right and cross the Hogsmill one last time, but look left carefully as soon as you have done so, otherwise you may miss the little iron gate, through which the Loop passes and descends steps for one final rendezvous with the Hogsmill. Look back now to discover the three stone arches of the late-12th-century bridge below today's road bridge – an amazing survival. A new walkway leads ahead across a brick-surfaced lane past Charter Square **[V]** to the point where the Hogsmill flows into the Thames. Now the Loop briefly joins the Thames Path National Trail (see page 20) by turning right along Charter Quay. If the sun is out, you may find it hard to believe that you are not somewhere on the Mediterranean.

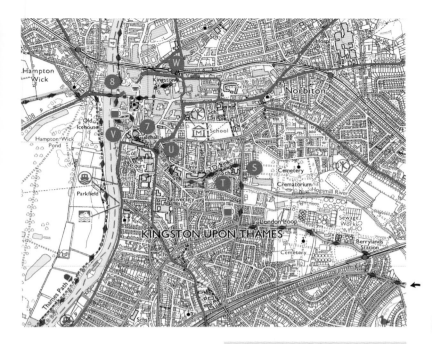

Pass two pubs, the Gazebo and the strangely named Bishop Out Of Residence, known locally simply as The Bishop. Ahead now is **Kingston Bridge [8]**, where Section 8 of the Loop ends.

> The present bridge opened in 1828 and was widened in 1914, but there has been a bridge here since at least the 13th century, possibly earlier, and this has contributed to the town's strategic importance. It was the only bridge over the Thames between London and Staines until Putney Bridge opened in 1729.

To continue on to Section 9, climb the steps ahead and turn left across the bridge, but Kingston's town centre is well worth exploring.

Link to Kingston Station (0.6 km/0.4 miles). Turn right up the slope and keep ahead along Clarence Street to the road corner, served by many bus routes 🚌. (Toilets on the first floor of John Lewis opposite.) Continue into the pedestrian precinct, passing the Bentalls Centre, to a crossing marked by a tiled 'three fishes' design in the pavement. Turn left along Fife Road, which bends right and later left to reach a light-controlled pedestrian crossing with Kingston station **[W]** opposite 🚆. There are, of course, many pubs, cafés and other facilities in the town centre.

9 Kingston Bridge to Hatton

14.9 km/9.3 miles plus links from Kingston station (0.6 km/0.4 miles) and to Hatton Cross station (1 km/0.6 miles). You can leave the route at Fulwell after 6.4 km/4 miles or several bus stops as described.

Cafés at Kingston, Bushy Park and Baber Bridge. Pub at Hanworth Road. Toilets at Kingston, Bushy Park and Hatton Cross (automatic). Best picnic opportunities: Bushy Park and Crane Park.

Local authorities: London Boroughs of Richmond-upon-Thames and Hounslow.

This almost entirely level section starts with glorious walking on grass and tracks through the heath and woodland of royal Bushy Park, where you are likely to see deer. A rather long stretch along residential roads follows to reach the greenery of another of London's lesser known rivers, the Crane, breaking off for an interesting diversion across Hounslow Heath.

Link from Kingston Station

(0.6 km/0.4 miles). From the station exit **[A]**, go ahead to cross at the pedestrian lights and keep ahead into Fife Road, which soon swings right and later left past the Bentall Centre. You reach the pedestrianised shopping area and turn right at the tiled 'three fishes' design in the pavement. Continue past John Lewis (toilets), with the parish church and turnings to Market Place on your left, and keep ahead on to the left-hand pavement of Kingston Bridge to rejoin the Loop.

Section 7 of the London Loop starts by crossing Kingston Bridge **[B]** on its left-hand pavement – keep left as the lower track on your right is for cyclists. On the far side is Hampton Wick, now in the London Borough of Richmond-upon-Thames, bear left at the roundabout **[C]** along the A308 Hampton Court Road. On your left

is the recessed Kingston Gate, which leads into the Home Park of Hampton Court Palace, but the Loop continues ahead to the Old King's Head pub where you cross at traffic lights then keep ahead along Church Grove beside a brick wall. Pass a gate into The King's Field then, opposite St John's Church, turn left through the narrow iron Church Grove Gate, one of the entry points into **Bushy Park [1]**. It leads into Church Grove Passage, an impressive avenue of horse chestnuts.

Bushy was one of three parks enclosed by Cardinal Wolsey as part of his Hampton Court estate and given to Henry VIII along with the palace. It was opened to the public in 1837 and is still grazed by deer, with occasional tree plantations to preserve its park-like quality. **Deer Warning**. Red and fallow deer roam freely throughout Bushy Park. Take heed of the warning notices. It is dangerous to approach the deer at any time. Feeding or touching the deer is prohibited – you should go no closer than 50 metres. This applies especially in May, June and July, when the females are protecting their young, and in September and October during the rutting and mating season. Dogs must be kept under close control at all times, otherwise they may be attacked by the deer, but if a deer chases you should let the dog run away.

Go through a much larger gate into the park itself, where you will be walking for the next 4.7 km/3 miles. Keep ahead on the broad track for 50 metres, then branch right to follow a worn path over grass to the corner **[D]** of the Cricket Field, beside its practice nets. Turn right along a grit track beside the fence to the next corner, near the entrance into Millennium Wood. To your left now is a vast expanse of rough, tussocky acid grassland, where skylarks nest – this is probably the nearest place to London where these soaring

songsters can still be found. Dogs should be kept out of this area.

When the track swings right, turn sharp left along a mown grass path through the tussocks to reach a seven-way junction of similar paths, with a Loop waymark post. Go half right through bracken towards the right-hand edge of the Oval Plantation to reach Leg of Mutton Pond **[2]** just beyond the trees. The path swings left to cross a low brick bridge over a channel flowing into the pond, where you turn left along its right bank. At a sandy track, turn right to skirt the larger Heron Pond **[3]**, which is fringed by some grand old weeping willow trees. At an especially widely spread one, where the track swings right, keep ahead on grass to stay beside the pond. You pass another willow that, despite having been knocked over, is clearly still very much alive. You come to a grit track by a criss-cross wooden footbridge **[E]**, where the Loop continues ahead. *However, if you wish to visit the famous Diana Fountain [4], 350 metres away, cross the bridge*

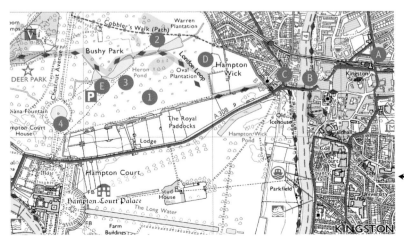

and follow the track through a car park, with a café and toilets.

After crossing the grit track, keep ahead on grass, now with another water channel to your left, known as the Taxodium River after a type of conifer. As it disappears beneath a white railing, go half left between trees to pass a huge old iron handpump on a plinth. On reaching Chestnut Avenue **[F]** beside a Loop waymark post, the shining bronze Diana Fountain can be seen away to your left, with **Hampton Court Palace [5]** beyond. In truth, only the nearest rows to the avenue are chestnut, the outer rows are limes. Cross the avenue, noting that traffic uses it, and bear slightly left through trees past two low white posts to reach a seat and another white railing, where the water channel reappears. Now you can see that it flows out beneath a fence ahead, which surrounds the Woodland Gardens – a great sickle-shaped swathe of trees that dominates the western half of the park.

Join a broad, sandy track among grassy tussocks left of the channel and follow it around to the right through a gate **[G]** in the fence. The gate leads into the **Pheasantry Plantation [6]**, the first section of the woodlands. *Over to your right, across a wooden footbridge, are a café and toilets.*

Note that, whereas most of Bushy Park is open 24 hours, these woodlands normally open between 8 and 9 am and close half an hour before dusk. If you should find them closed you can follow the fence to your left, turn right along

the Ash Walk **[H]** between two parts of the woodland, then go left again beside the fence to rejoin the route at point **[J]**.

The Loop turns left inside the gate, along a grit path that meanders through the manicured woodland, taking a left then a right fork in the process, but always keeping near the watercourse to your right, here known as the Keeper's River. By the water's edge rises perhaps the strangest growth around the entire Loop – the aerial roots of a swamp cypress, their jagged stumps pointing skywards like a dentist's nightmare. Over to your right appears a pretty cottage, Keeper's Lodge, surely one of the most idyllic dwellings in the whole of London.

Wooden gates take you across a strip that divides the woodlands and carries a main park route, the Ash Walk **[H]**. Cross straight over to enter the next part, the **Waterhouse Plantation [7]**, through another gate beside a little 'sentry hut'. Keep ahead on the main path, forking right at two points, to reach a T-junction. Turn right to follow the straight Macclesfield Walk along the right-hand side of the third section of the woodlands, the Willow Plantation, passing River Lodge **[I]**. Unlike the previous beautifully kept garden-like areas, this one has been deliberately left unkempt to benefit wildlife – the naturalists' version of organised chaos.

At the end, a wooden gate leads on to a tarmac crossing track called Cobblers Walk, named after Timothy Bennet, shoemaker of Hampton Wick, who established it as a right of way across the park. *An optional 60-metre leftward diversion here takes you to the Longford River [8], a 19 km/12 mile artificial waterway that was created during the 17th century to bring fresh water from the River Colne to Bushy Park and Hampton Court.* Turn right along Cobblers Walk, through another gate [J], back into the open parkland, and immediately turn left to follow an earth track beside a fence. You join a main path, which swings right as you approach **Upper Lodge [9]**.

Take a left fork over grass to join and turn left along the metalled Upper Lodge Road, which is used by vehicles. As the road swings left, bear slightly right along a tarmac path to cross

another one, with a little willow-fringed pond over to your left. Surely with much reluctance, Loop walkers must now leave Bushy Park through its Laurel Road Gate [K], to follow residential roads for a while. Keep ahead along a grit path to come beside Laurel Road itself, leading to the A313 Hampton Road on the fringe of Teddington. 🚌
From the stop this side on your right to Hampton Court, Feltham and Hatton Cross; from the far side on your left to Twickenham, Richmond and Kingston.
Use the pedestrian lights to your left to cross over and keep ahead along Kings Road, then take the first left, which brings you to the A311 [L] – Hampton Hill High Street to your left, Wellington Road to your right.

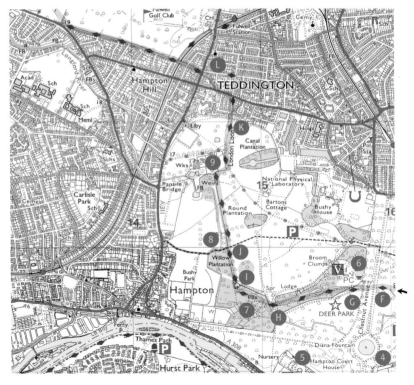

Link with Fulwell station (0.5 km/0.3 miles). Turn right along Wellington Road, past a church, to Clonmel Road where you turn right then bear left down a footpath beside the railway, which leads to the station **[M]. Returning from the station**, turn left at the top of steps from the platform, then right along a footpath beside the railway. Keep on to the main road and turn left, then cross over at pedestrian lights and continue on the opposite pavement to Burtons Road, where you turn right to rejoin the Loop.

There is no pedestrian crossing here, so if traffic is heavy use the lights to your left. Cross over to keep ahead along the left-hand pavement of the long and straight Burtons Road for 1 km/0.6 miles, soon crossing a railway bridge **[N]**. At last it swings left to reach the A312 Uxbridge Road, where you ignore the Loop signs opposite and turn right to cross Burtons Road, then immediately right again through a green metal fence **[O]** to follow a dirt path into the scrubland of Fulwell Park.

Soon fork right to go along the left-hand edge of a playing field, then at its end bear left along a mown grass path that links to a grit path between fences. On your left now is a David Lloyd sports club, and as the main path swings right to its car park you keep ahead on a narrower path to cross the drive then go through a gate **[P]** to reach the A305 (Twickenham Road to the left, Staines Road to the right). Turn right past the sports club's vehicle entrance, then cross at the pedestrian lights to continue on the far side. 🚍 *From the stop on*

this side for Feltham, Hatton Cross and Heathrow, also (non-TfL) Sunbury and Staines; far side for Twickenham and Richmond.

In 330 metres turn left along Court Close Avenue **[Q]**, then comes a quick sequence of turns in quiet residential roads: right (Rivermeads Avenue), left (Bye Ways) and right (Willow Way). This brings you to the much busier B358 Hospital Bridge Road, where you turn left to cross Hospital Bridge **[R]** itself, over the River Crane.

You can see the riverside path we want below but to reach it you must walk on to a gate, turn left into Crane Park, then immediately fork left off the tarmac path to drop down a broad, mown grass path through a wildflower meadow. Join the tarmac path beside the **River Crane [10]** to go under the A316 Chertsey Road on a dark causeway, but take care as this is a shared use track and there's not much room here for walkers and cyclists. Keep ahead but soon fork left to follow an earth path beside the river, cutting a corner off the tarmac one. It can be quite dark under the trees, so watch out for exposed roots.

Soon a parallel tangle of boulders and branches speeds the river's flow around a bend, then another left fork keeps you on the earth path beside the water. A seat that is covered with carved wooden insects provides a suitable spot to sit and admire a photogenic bend in the river, though the sound of aircraft landing at Heathrow may be something of a distraction. Suddenly a great brick structure, the **Shot Tower [11]** (see page 92) appears through the trees ahead.

Now the Loop turns away from the river by going behind the tower to rejoin the tarmac path by an information board. Take the right fork, through a grass area with two seats and ignoring a right turn, to reach a little barbecue area with plenty of seating for a picnic. Leave the park through a gate **[S]** and turn right along the A314 Hanworth Road. We must now make a diversion rightwards, starting with a rather long walk beside the A314 for 1 km/0.6 miles, keeping to the right-hand pavement at first.

From this side to Hampton and Kingston; far side to Hounslow and Heathrow Central.

Keep on to the Duke of York pub and shops, then cross at the pedestrian lights to continue along the far side past Hounslow Cemetery and over a railway bridge. Cross Simpson Road **[T]** then very soon, at a low white railing,

turn left on grass across a playing field, with a playground over to your right. Keep ahead through trees to cross a stile then turn right on a sandy shared-use track, which leads into both the open vistas of **Hounslow Heath [12]** and appropriately enough the London Borough of Hounslow.

"Across the untamed heath you can still conjure up images of days when highwaymen and footpads gave the heath its evil reputation, and the coach road across it was lined with rotting corpses on gibbets, swinging and rattling their chains in the harsh wind. I hope I'm not putting you off!" *David Sharp*

Follow the broad grit track ahead for 260 metres to reach a lonely little bench, where you fork left on a mown grass path through scrub. Pass another

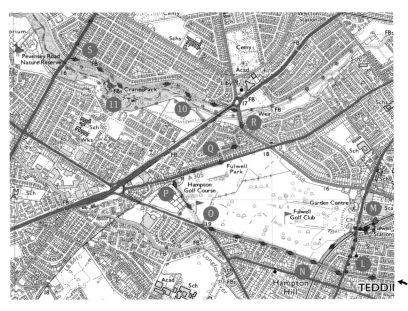

bench at a cross-tracks to continue ahead beside a barbed wire fence and keep on when it swings right. Soon turn right along a rough track that follows the edge of the public heath, with Hounslow Heath Golf Course to your left. At a junction **[U]** just before a large area of open ground, fork left on a narrow grass path through shrubbery, which shortly goes left through a barrier, then left again. Ignore a rise to your left to continue ahead on a path through a gully between golf fairways. When this rises to cross a golfers' track, keep ahead on grass to go right of a disused tee. Follow a track that leads down to a bridge over an old millstream, then fork right on a narrow path to rejoin the River Crane across another bridge **[V]**.

Turn right then walk upstream, with the river to your right and an old pumping station on your left. Approaching some houses, fork right and soon cross a wooden bridge over a side stream, now in Brazil Mill Woods. You pass an old, overgrown bridge to come beside garden fences, then after the river divides into two channels around an island, fork right to stay beside the river. A larger bridge appears ahead – Baber Bridge **[W]**, carrying the A315, another Staines Road. Just before it, the path goes left to reach the road through a veritable chicane of a green metal barrier. This road is very busy with a blind bend to your right, so turn left to cross at the lights. *There is a café and food shops here.* 🚌 *From the stops on this side to Feltham (also non-TfL Staines and Sunbury); from the far side to Hounslow and Isleworth.*

After crossing at the lights, come back on the far side past Roman Close then go left through a barrier into **Donkey Wood [13]**. Keep to the main path as it crosses a sluice, then

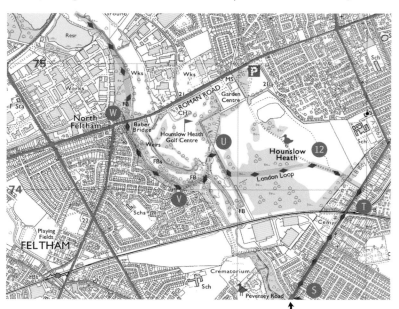

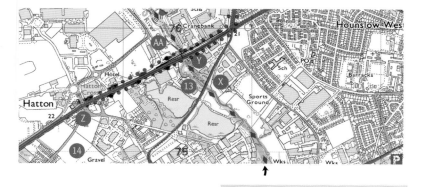

goes via a footbridge over a millrace – this is not the Crane but the Duke of Northumberland's River, another artificial watercourse, this one cut in the 16th century to provide power for watermills. The path wanders on past a junction and through woodland ahead for some time before rejoining the Crane just before the ruins of an old working shed, with its high blast shield bank. Keep these to your left as you continue to reach a long and winding timber causeway along a particularly boggy stretch of riverside – take care as it can be slippery when wet and is a little wonky in places. Cross a footbridge over a side channel then walk beside a high green security fence, behind which is a nature reserve that is actually part of the vast territory of **Heathrow Airport [14]**, which stretches away to your left for over 6.5 km/4 miles.

The path goes under A312 The Causeway **[X]**, but then climbs steps to the far side of the road. Turn left at the top, over the Crane, then immediately left again along a grit path through Causeway Water Meadows, a small nature reserve. Section 9 of the Loop comes to an abrupt end when you encounter the thunderous traffic on the A30 Great South-West Road at Hatton **[Y]**.

If you are finishing your day's walk here, the tedious but practical thing to do is turn left along the shared use track beside the A30 for 0.9 km/0.6 miles to the traffic lights, go right across three sets of lights, then turn left to cross four more sets of lights to **Hatton Court station [Z]** ⊖ (Piccadilly Line) 🚌 (buses in all directions). You may be able to take a bus part of the way.

If you want to walk further along the Loop, though the continuation is just 70 metres away on the far side of the A30, there is no way across and you must make a diversion of 1 km/0.6 miles. Turn right along the shared-use track beside the A30 to traffic lights at the junction with A312 The Causeway. Cross left over four carriageways then go right, beside a fence, to an entrance into the Heathrow Estate. Turn left and left again to follow a tarmac path down to Earhart Way. Shortly cross over to continue on a pavement along the far side, parallel with the A30 and passing three entrances into commercial premises. In 350 metres, when the road rises a little to cross the Crane, turn right past two barriers **[AA]** to rejoin the Loop.

10 Hatton to Hayes & Harlington

6.5 km/4 miles plus links from Hatton Cross station (1 km/0.6 miles) and to Hayes & Harlington station (0.2 km/0.1 miles). You can leave the route at several bus stops as described.

Cafés at Hayes. Pubs at North Hyde Road and Hayes. No public toilets on this section. Best picnic opportunities at Cranebank, Cranford Country Park and Cranford stables yard.

Local authorities: London Boroughs of Hounslow and Hillingdon.

The route is mostly level as it continues beside the River Crane then through Berkeley Meadows and Cranford Country Park to join the Grand Union Canal.

Link from Hatton Cross station (1 km/0.6 miles). Leave the station **[A]** (automatic toilet) by its Great South-West Road exit and turn left to cross a road ahead at four sets of traffic lights. Keep on in this direction for 350 metres, beside the A30, remembering that this is a shared-use pavement. Reaching a high concrete wall that conceals Piccadilly Line trains below, follow the pavement to the left of it, pass a roundabout and continue past a barrier along Earhart Way, parallel to the A30. Cross the River Crane then turn left past two barriers **[B]** to rejoin the Loop.

"You start this section of the Loop accompanied by the roar of aircraft engines, admiring the jumbo jets as they come in to land, seemingly within touching distance, and end it with the sleepy thump-thump of a canal narrow boat – sounds that are truly centuries apart." *David Sharp*

This first section beside the Crane between points **[B]** and **[D]** is liable to flooding after heavy rain, and the London Borough of Hounslow has been asked to remedy this. If you are unable to get through, unfortunately the only action currently available is to use our map to navigate your way around the roads between these points.

After its enforced break, the Loop continues through two barriers **[B]** on a stony path in the **Cranebank [1]** section of the River Crane Park, frequently passing seats. As the name suggests, the meandering, reed-filled river is close by to your left, though mostly hidden by greenery. The path veers left by a gate to pass grazing land and reach another barrier **[C]**, where you fork left across a playing field. You come to a grass strip that follows the river ahead, but at present this is a dead end, so you must follow the grit path as it swings right to pass a children's playground. Turn left to leave the meadows via a third barrier between houses and reach Waye Avenue, then turn left to follow it around two bends to a junction **[D]**, where turn left again to reach the A4, here called Bath Road but actually the ancient Great West Road that connected the City of London with Bristol. *There are food shops and a café here.* 🚌 *From the stop to your left on this side to Hayes & Harlington, West Drayton, Uxbridge and Heathrow Central.*

Cross the A4 at the traffic lights just to your right. 🚌 *From the stop to your right to Hounslow East and West, Southall, Greenford, Hampton and Kingston.* Turn left along the shared-use pavement to cross Cranford's modest High Street and walk a further

200 metres to cross the balustraded Cranford Bridge **[E]** into the London Borough of Hillingdon. Here was the ford over the Crane that gave Cranford its name, and the bridge still proudly carries the shield of the now-departed County of Middlesex. Where the railings end, go sharp right under an arch to join a dirt path through the open grass of Berkeley Meadows, with the Crane now behind trees over to your right. The path winds past a children's playground to reach Cranford Lane **[F]**, which you cross then turn right, keeping close to the left-hand side with great care as there is no pavement and traffic comes blind around the bend.

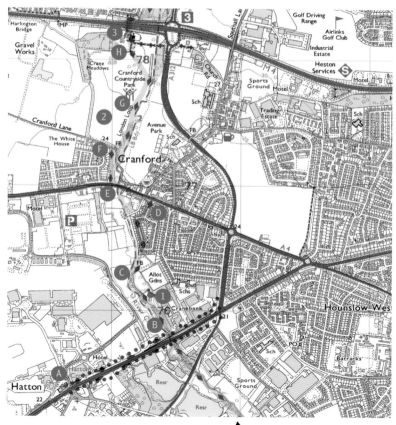

In 40 metres turn left over a raised concrete kerb into woodland, then immediately fork right on an earth path to cross a plank bridge. Shortly turn left at a path junction, with the Crane now to your right, to follow a broad, grassy track in a beech copse along the edge of **Cranford Country Park [2]**, once the estate of the Earls of Berkeley. At a junction **[G]** with a mown path, keep ahead into the park's open grassland, passing a seat, then in 80 metres fork right at a waymark post to go back into the trees along a mown grass path. This leads to a bend in a sandy path, but ignore that and bear half left, back into the open field, aiming for the left end of a fenced enclosure ahead, which contains a children's playground with picnic tables. At a fingerpost **[H]** on the corner, go slightly right between the fence and another ha-ha (see page 30). Go ahead to the fence beyond the car park and turn left, past **St Dunstan's Church [3]**.

A gate leads into the delightful cobbled yard of the stable blockyard, where you pass a ring of hedges containing seats arranged in a circle – a lovely spot for a picnic. The Loop is joined here by the Hillingdon Trail, which does its borough proud by carving a route of no less than 31 km/19 miles from end to end. The two routes march together out of the yard by turning right through the further archway of the stables. For some time, you will have been made noisily aware that there's a busy thoroughfare ahead: it's the M4 motorway, and you go under it through St Dunstan's Subway **[I]**.

Turn right on the far side, following a grit bridleway near the motorway for a while, then soon forking left into the woodland of Dog Kennel Covert, still in Cranford Country Park. Soon the thunder of the M4 gives way to the twitter of songbirds as you continue along the track, ignoring a sign taking the Hillingdon Trail briefly rightwards, and others trying to tempt you on to a nature trail. Ahead rises a huge brown-brick telephone exchange, surmounted by a tall aerial. Coming to a green gate, keep ahead along Watersplash Lane to reach traffic lights at North Hyde Road **[J]** beside the Crane pub. 🚌 *From stops to your left, this side for Hayes & Harlington; far side for Southall, Boston Manor and Brentford.*

Turn right to follow the right-hand pavement over the Crane to a big roundabout, then left across two sets of traffic lights, going left of a grey transformer cabinet on the far side. Ignore a track that leads down to a subway and go over grass to join a tarmac shared-use track that goes off to the right, beside a fence. It soon swings left to go join a cycle track for a mercifully brief stretch beside the dual carriageway A312 The Parkway, with the Crane now hidden among trees down to your left. All these thoroughfares climb purposefully, and you soon realise that you are crossing the **Grand Union Canal [4]**. Turn left through a gap to start a 200-metre trek down a ramp **[K]** which has many twists and turns.

The ramp is surfaced in two shades of tarmac: grey for pedestrians and red for cyclists. In truth, the towpath is too narrow for shared use in places, so you will need to be more alert than usual to cyclists coming from behind, and when you go under bridges bear in mind the possibility that one may come around a blind bend ahead.

Before turning right at the foot of the ramp, a brief diversion leftwards is worth taking for a closer look at the gleaming white **Bull's Bridge [5]**, where the Grand Union's branch to Paddington Basin starts.

At the foot of the ramp, turn right along the towpath to go under the A312, and take note that the number 204 appears on a little plate attached to the bridge. All canal bridges are numbered thus – they provide a good guide to where you have got to on an otherwise featureless towpath and we refer to them here. Look down for one last sighting of the River Crane, before going under a service road

(203) and bridge 202 carrying Brunel's **Great Western Railway [6]** from Paddington to the West Country and Wales. The next bridge (201) **[L]** is for Station Road, where the Old Crown pub lies up to your right and Section 10 of the Loop ends.

To continue on to Section 11, keep ahead under bridge 200.

Link to Hayes & Harlington Station (250 metres). Turn right up the steps to the Old Crown, then turn left to Station Road. Hayes town centre (note that this is often referred to as Hayes Middlesex to distinguish it from the one known as Hayes Kent) lies to your right with cafés and food shops, but the link now turns left again to pass a mini-roundabout and keep ahead up the slope to the station **[M]** (no toilets).

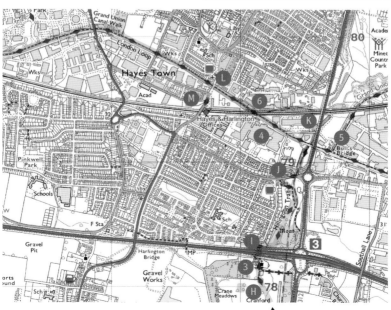

Hayes & Harlington to Uxbridge

10.9 km/7.8 miles plus links from Hayes & Harlington station (0.2 km/0.1 miles and to Uxbridge station (0.7 km/0.4 miles). You can leave the route at West Drayton after 4.6 km/2.9 miles or several bus stops as described.

Cafés at Hayes, Yiewsley and West Drayton. Pubs at Dawley Road, Yiewsley, West Drayton, Clisby's Bridge, Uxbridge Moor and Uxbridge. Toilets at Yiewsley and West Drayton. Best picnic opportunities at Stockley Park and Little Britain Lake.

Local authorities: London Borough of Hillingdon, Buckinghamshire County Council (South Bucks District).

The Loop continues along the Grand Union Canal towpath into Uxbridge, but makes two expeditions into outstanding open spaces nearby: first climbing into one of London's lesser known large open spaces, Stockley Park, then beside the River Colne to follow the shore of idyllic Little Britain Lake.

Link from Hayes & Harlington station (200 metres, no toilets). From the station exit **[A]** turn right down Station Road and past the roundabout to the canal bridge. There are cafés and food shops in Hayes town centre further along Station Road, but for the Loop turn right by the Old Crown pub along Western View then go down steps and keep ahead on the towpath under the bridge **[B]** to rejoin the Loop.

Walk under bridge 200 **[B]** and past the 'GJC' 87-mile post. Soon you go under three more bridges: two quite modern ones (199 **[C]**, Printing House

Lane, and 198 **[D]**, A437 Dawley Road with the Woolpack pub nearby), then the older 196, almost hidden by trees, which carries an old track leading to a commercial estate with a weekday café. Bridge 197 was apparently surplus to requirements. When the trees that line the canal here are in full leaf, they mask the surrounding industry so well that you could be forgiven for thinking that you are deep in the countryside. Soon a bench and a reedy inlet (a former dock) **[E]** appear on your right behind railings, just before mile post 86, and the Loop now abandons the canal for a while to do a little exploring.

Turn right up a sandy path, which passes through a complex steel gate then winds through shrubbery to reach a brown-brick tiled road called Furzeground Way. You are now in **Stockley Park [1]**, and you realise that the former dock has been turned into a pleasant water feature for the benefit of staff in the nearby hi-tech offices. 🚌 *From the stop to your*

left on this side to West Drayton and Heathrow Central; from the stop to your right on the far side to Hayes & Harlington and Uxbridge.

Follow the yellow bricks across the road then turn left on a footway along the far side. In 35 metres turn right along a grass verge beside a depot driveway, then in 20 metres turn right again along a gravel track. Soon turn left along a shared use track, which briefly divides into two carriageways between lines of trees, where you should keep right. At a more open spot, with a golf fairway on your right, take a left fork, still tree-lined. Shortly fork right to pass an occasional car park, then bear left on grass beside a drive to reach a Loop main sign. *Up to your right now is Stockley Pines [F], the club-house of Stockley Park Golf Club, whose café*

and toilets are open to the public.

Before the drive enters the car park, bear right up a grit track that climbs steadily, at first between steps leading to the club-house, then in a gully between golf fairways. It leads eventually to an unusual bridge [G], suspended from a single pylon, linking the two halves of Stockley Park on either side of the dual carriageway A408 Stockley Road. There are golf holes on both sides too, so give a cheery wave to the many golfers who use the bridge as you cross over, using the right-hand walkway. Take the broad track ahead, ignoring turnings to those golf holes. *At the top, as you draw breath, it's worth climbing a little further up a mound to your right, for the magnificent 360-degree panoramic view, with three benches providing a grand spot for a picnic.*

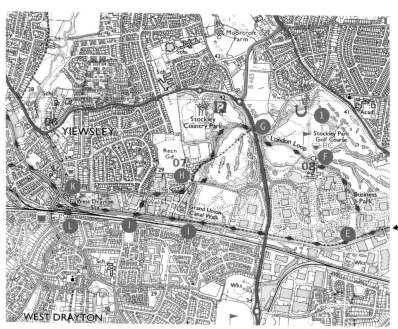

As you start to descend, fork left off the main track over a grassy area, through a gap in bushes and more grass, to reach another fork in trees. Keep left, soon coming alongside a horseride on your left, with a car park beyond the trees on your right. As the track swings left, turn right on a narrow path through trees and a gate **[H]** to leave Stockley Park on to Horton Road. 🚌 *From the stop on this side to Hayes & Harlington; on the far side (around to your right) to West Drayton and Heathrow Central.*

The Loop now uses a new path that has been constructed here to avoid a long and tedious stretch beside roads. Cross over and turn right a few paces, then go through a gate on your left to climb a path up to and along an embankment. At the far end, steps take you back down to the Grand Union Canal towpath **[I]**, where you turn right. On the far bank now, through an array of gantries, speed trains of the Great Western Railway and the Heathrow Express, and joining them from 2019 those of the Elizabeth Line, originally known as Crossrail 1. You pass mile post 85 then go under Horton Bridge (193) **[J]**. The canal swings right ahead to reach Colham Bridge (192) **[K]**, adorned on either side by a shiny stainless steel arch, where the link with West Drayton station starts.

Link with West Drayton Station
(200 metres). Turn right past a swan motif in the brickwork, walk up the cobbled slope, then turn left to reach two High Streets. To your left is that of West Drayton, with the train 🚆 and bus 🚌 stations **[L]** (toilets, a café and the De Burgh Arms pub). To your right,

that of Yiewsley, with cafés, food stores, an automatic toilet and the George & Dragon pub. **Returning from the rail station**, turn left to the High Street, where turn right for 100 metres. Cross the canal, immediately turn right (Horton Road), then right again down the slope to the towpath **[K]**, and right a third time to rejoin the Loop.

The Loop continues under the bridge, soon reaching bridge 191 (Trout Road), beyond which is a popular mooring for narrowboats and a series of long benches. Next comes a big Tesco and shortly after that a criss-cross girder bridge **[M]**, which seems to have been slotted in late as it carries the number 190B. You have reached another location that is very well known to canal boaters: Cowley Peachy Junction, with the **Packet Boat Marina [2]** just ahead. *The Packet Boat pub can be reached in 0.5 km/0.3 miles by continuing ahead to the next bridge then turn right up the road.*

But the Loop now climbs the cobbled slope to cross this steeply humped old bridge and follow the tranquil **Slough Arm [3]** of the Grand Union, just about the last canal to be built in this country, in 1885. It runs virtually straight for 8 km/5 miles, but we only stay with it for half a mile (750 metres).

Walk under a footbridge that serves the marina: just to confuse us, its number is '0' – perhaps it was a late addition after number 1 had been built. Soon a short cast-iron aqueduct **[N]** with curving brick walls takes the canal over the 8-km/5-mile long Fray's River, thought to be an artifical watercourse created in the 15th century by John Fray, the Chancellor of the Exchequer of his day – a mill stream on a grand scale! Immediately past this is a blocked-up concrete **pillbox [4]** then a ramshackle warehouse.

> Some 18,000 pillboxes were constructed throughout the UK (but mainly in south-east England) during World Wars I and II as guard posts against invading troops. The name comes from their similarity in shape to boxes that used to be provided by pharmacists for medicinal pills.

Soon you reach another criss-cross girder bridge (number 1) **[O]** where the Loop leaves the Slough Arm. Go under it then immediately turn left, passing a **coal-tax post [5]**.

Turn left again at the top to cross the bridge, and you'll notice that it seems rather substantial for a footpath – this is because it once carried a light goods railway. We follow its track through some rather wild woodland and around two quite tight bends to emerge suddenly at a small car park beside willow-girt **Little Britain Lake [6]** – a former gravel pit but now perhaps one of the most delightful spots encountered by the Loop, with several benches along its shore. Apparently it got this name from the vague resemblance of its shape to the island of Great Britain. To your left is a little shingle beach, up which laps water from the River Colne beyond. A place in which to linger awhile, if you blank out the roar of traffic on the M25, some 500 metres to the west. You are now well and truly inside the **Colne Valley Park [7]**, which was created in 1965 to provide a green lung for west London, and the Loop stays beside or close to the river for the next 11 km/7 miles or so.

There are toilets 200 metres to your right along the lake shore.

Tearing yourself away from this idyll, take the tarmac path that starts off to your left but then realises its mistake and hurriedly swings right. At a gate **[P]**, ignore the path ahead and cross a narrow footbridge over the Colne, then turn right to follow the river's left bank along an earth path among shrubs and trees, with the farmland of Huntsmoor Park to your left. Occasionally straying into Buckinghamshire, the path crosses several side streams and passes two footpath junctions, while in the river are the scant remains of an old mill, a pretty weir **[Q]** and a great spread of water lilies. At a gate, turn right then climb steps **[R]** to reach the B470 Iver Lane – but take great care, checking both ways before you step out, then cross over and turn right along the pavement on the far side.

Cross back over the Crane on Clisby's Bridge, with the remarkable sight of a forest of blue 'cherry pickers' (elevated work platforms) in the industrial park to your left. *Some 200 metres ahead, over a canal bridge, is the Malt Shovel pub.* Where the bridge railings end, turn sharply left on to a stony path that continues beside the river, soon meeting a gate and a wooden sculpture that depicts this part of the Colne Valley Park – it even shows the

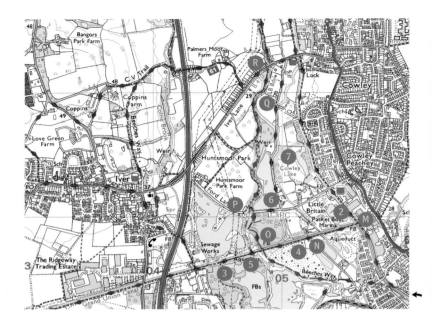

Loop's route. For 400 metres the path squeezes between the river and a high, slightly intimidating green fence, but persevere as the river has some charming stretches.

Eventually the fence ends and the path continues beside scrubland and beneath power lines. You pass a green barrier **[S]** at a timber yard, then swing right, away from the river and past another of those Colne Valley Park sculptures. Across a side stream appears the pleasant little garden of the West London Community College for autistic children. At a barrier, keep ahead along a road (Longbridge Way) through a commercial estate, in a district known as Uxbridge Moor, with the stream on your left, then you can soon use the pavement on the right-hand side to reach busy Cowley Mill Road **[T]**. Cross over to continue almost directly ahead along Culvert

Lane, which has no pavement but is very quiet. It leads past Church Lane and back to the Grand Union Canal, where you turn left along the towpath, with houses and gardens on your left. This is another very popular mooring area, with Hillingdon Canal Club on the far bank, and some sizeable converted barges amongst the narrowboats.

The pretty General Elliott pub appears on the left bank, behind its white fence, then carrying the A4007 Rockingham Road comes bridge 186 **[U]**, known as Dolphin Bridge after the pub of that name on its far side. An ultramodern domed building opposite – surely intended as an arts centre or theatre – has been commandeered by a sign works. Ahead, a little bridge that cowers beneath some hulking great office blocks is significant for us as it marks the end of Section 11 of the Loop. It's bridge number 185 **[V]** carrying the A4020 Oxford Road – go through to the foot of a ramp outside the Swan & Bottle pub in Uxbridge.

To continue on to Section 12, keep ahead along the towpath.

The historic Crown & Treaty pub **[8]** is just 100 metres away across the bridge. With its mellow brick frontage and Jacobean gabled end, it was originally a mansion called Place House, where in 1645 during the English Civil War the Commissioners of Charles I met Parliament to try to negotiate a treaty. After twenty days of debate they parted, with no treaty agreed, and the war rumbled on for another six years. Around 1800 what remained of their meeting house was converted into the inn you see today.

Link to Uxbridge station
(0.7 km/0.4 miles). Climb the ramp to the pub car park, then go left up some steps and left again over the canal. Follow the A4020 Oxford Road a short distance, with the Crown & Treaty pub over the road, cross Sanderson Road at three-stage traffic lights then shortly bear left up the High Street. Cross Harefield Road at a zebra crossing, then Belmont Road diagonally at traffic lights, and continue into the pedestrianised town centre, passing several pubs and cafés and the Pavilions shopping mall, to find the tube station **[W]** ⊖ (Piccadilly and Metropolitan Lines) on your left, with the bus station next to it.

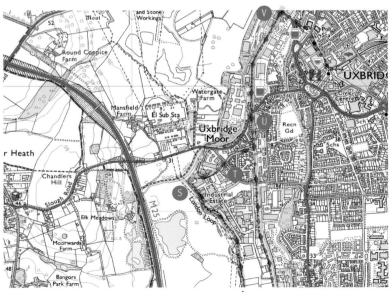

12 Uxbridge to Harefield West

7.7 km/4.8 miles plus links 0.7 km/0.4 miles from Uxbridge station and 0.2 km/0.1 miles to the bus stop in Harefield West. You can leave the route at South Harefield after 4.8 km/3 miles.

Cafés at Uxbridge, Denham Lock, Denham Country Park (0.6 km/0.4 miles off route) and Widewater. Pubs at Widewater and Coppermill Bridge. Toilets at Uxbridge station and Denham Country Park (0.6 km/0.4 miles) off route. Best picnic opportunities at Frays Valley Nature Reserve and Black Jack's Lock.

Local authorities: London Borough of Hillingdon, Buckinghamshire (South Bucks District).

More of the Grand Union Canal as the Loop heads northwards, almost completely level and mostly on firm paths and tracks. The Loop leaves the towpath for a while to pass two large lakes and nature reserves.

Link from Uxbridge station (0.7 km/0.4 miles, toilets and cafés in station concourse; from the bus station go through the underground station concourse). From the main exit **[A]** turn right along the pedestrianised High Street, past the Pavilions shopping mall, then cross Belmont Road diagonally at traffic lights and continue in the same direction, still the High Street. Cross Harefield Road at a zebra crossing then drop down across Sanderson Road via three-stage traffic lights and continue along the A3020 Oxford Road over the canal bridge to reach the Swan & Bottle pub. Go down a few steps into the pub car park, then immediately turn right down a ramp **[B]** and rejoin the Loop by keeping ahead along the canal towpath.

Accompanied by the Colne Valley Trail and National Cycle Network route 6, the Loop continues along the towpath with the Parexel building opposite, on its ring of concrete stilts, the headquarters of a multinational pharmaceutical consultancy. Further along that bank is the entrance to **Denham Marina [1]**. Cross a humped bridge (number 184) to pass **Uxbridge Lock [2]**, then Uxbridge Alderglade, a nature reserve.

The River Colne flows in from the left to feed the canal, then a quartet of sewage pipes leads you under bridge 183a **[C]**. With rough pasture on either side now, follow the towpath over the next bridge (183), a humped traditional canal brick arch, and on to **Denham Lock [3]**, beside which is the idyllic Fran's Tea Garden. *Just before Denham Lock, a path to your left leads in 0.6 km/0.4 miles to the visitor centre of Denham Country Park, which has a café, toilets and a natural history exhibition.*

At the next bridge (182) **[D]**, a little iron girder affair, the towpath continues ahead, but the Loop's designers thought you might welcome a break from the canal at this point. Cross the steeply ramped bridge, taking care on the descent (especially if wet) and follow a path across a ditch into the **Frays Valley Nature Reserve [4]**, created from former gravel pits.

Turn left along a broad, cinder track in Denham Lock Wood, much used by anglers and their vehicles, passing a touching rustic memorial to Paddy Cash. The track swings left and right to pass under an eight-arch brick viaduct (bridge number 181) **[E]**, which carries Chiltern Line trains. Now you are back

beside the canal, though the towpath is on the opposite bank. The even bigger lake to your right is used by sailing dinghies from the Hillingdon Outdoor Activities Centre on the far shore.

The track swings right, past rows and rows of narrow boats crammed into Harefield Marina, to reach a junction **[F]**. Leave the main track to keep ahead on a lesser one, then in 90 metres at another junction turn left along a footpath to rejoin the original track. In 50 metres the Loop passes a metal farm gate then immediately turns off the track to follow a parallel footpath through trees. At a fork, keep

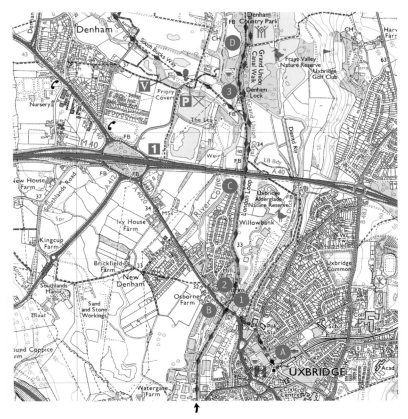

Uxbridge to Harefield West

ahead through a barrier then turn left to reach Moorhall Road in South Harefield. Your exit seems barred by concrete blocks **[G]**, but someone has taken a massive sledgehammer to bash a way through.

The Loop goes left along the pavement, with a commercial centre called Widewater Place opposite *(café and toilets, open Monday to Friday 6 am to 3 pm)*. Soon you come to a bridge **[H]** that takes you back over the canal, and rejoin the towpath by turning left down steps. *For the Bear on the Barge (formerly Horse & Barge) pub keep ahead for 90 metres.* 🚌 *From the stop on this side to Uxbridge (also Denham non-TfL); from the far side to Northwood and Ruislip.* Double back under bridge 180 to climb past Widewater Lock.

Back in dense tree cover again, the towpath continues to pass under bridge 179 **[I]**, and to your left you should catch glimpses of Broadwater Lake, another vast former gravel pit nature reserve used for saling. *A fine meadow climbs the hillside opposite to meet the Old Orchard pub – you can reach it after a stiff 350-metre climb from the bridge ahead, but soon there's another pub next to the canal.* Take care as you pass under bridge 178, which leads to **Black Jack's Lock [5]**, as cycles may appear suddenly and the towpath is narrow.

The Hillingdon Trail comes in from the right here to rejoin the Loop and the Colne Valley Trail for a while. The next length of towpath leads you over three footbridges. The first crosses the mill race, just before a tennis court, as

the houses of Harefield West appear on the far bank. The second passes a 'labyrynthine weir', designed to allow a greater flow of water in a confined space. The third **[J]** once allowed boats to pass through its arch into a wharf that served a mill, whose site is now occupied by a depot of the Clancy Docwra construction company.

Just a little further on you reach Coppermill Bridge (177), beside which stands the Coy Carp pub, formerly the Fisheries Inn. Now the Loop ends its on-off relationship with the Grand Union by crossing the narrow road bridge **[K]**, where you should take care and keep right in Coppermill Lane as

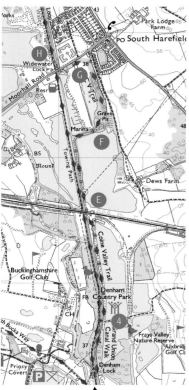

there's no pavement for 75 metres. Follow the road around two bends into Park Lane then cross over to use the pavement up the left-hand side past the entrance of Royal Quay, a large development of old and new buildings around the old Copper Mill, for both residential and commercial use. The adjacent grand house was once occupied by the mill-owner. Section 12 of the Loop ends at the junction **[L]** with Summerhouse Lane.

To continue on to Section 13, turn left along Summerhouse Lane.

For the bus to Uxbridge (the Sunday service is only hourly), continue up Park Lane for 200 metres, passing Barrington Drive, to reach a turning circle **[M]** with a smart embossed metal Loop information panel. The bus stops here on a spur route from Harefield village **[6]**, 1 km/0.6 miles away. The village can be reached on a roadside verge or pavement and has more frequent buses as well as several cafés and pubs, including the aforementioned Old Orchard.

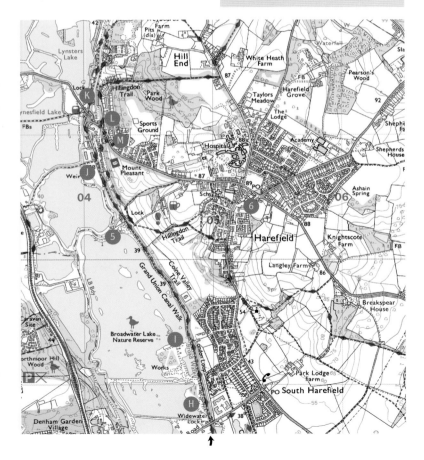

13 Harefield West to Moor Park

7.5 km/4.7 miles plus links 0.2 km/0.1 miles from Harefield West bus stop and 0.8 km/0.5 miles to Moor Park Station. You can leave the route at several bus stops as described.

Cafés at Harefield village and Moor Park. Pubs at Woodcock Hill and Batchworth Heath. Toilets at Moor Park station. Best picnic opportunities at Coppermill Lock and Bishop's Wood Country Park.

Local authorities: London Borough of Hillingdon, Hertfordshire County Council (Three Rivers District).

A stiff ascent starts off this section, then it's high, rolling Hertfordshire countryside all the way, much of it on earth (therefore possibly muddy) and grass paths and tracks, and ten stiles to negotiate. A long stretch through lovely Bishops Wood occupies the central part.

The U9 bus from Uxbridge makes a detour from Harefield village to the Belfry Avenue bus stop, actually at the turning circle **[A]** by Shelley Lane. Walk 200 metres down Park Lane to the junction with Summerhouse Lane **[B]** and turn right. There are more frequent services to Harefield village **[1]**, then it's a 1.2-km/0.7-mile walk down Park Lane. Note the smart Loop embossed metal information panel at the bus turning circle.

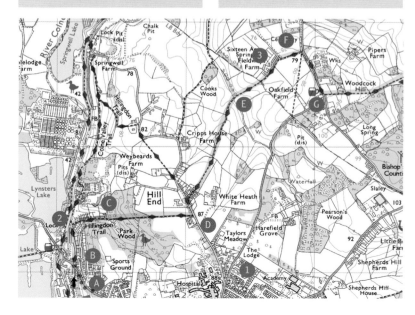

Walk along Summerhouse Lane with the Long Room on your left, one of the original buildings associated with the Copper Mill and now the home of several small information technology companies. At its end lie the moorings of the Hillingdon Narrowboats Association, whose interesting history is described online at www.hna.org.uk. Just a few steps across their cobbles allows a pleasant view of **Coppermill Lock [2]**.

> The big mills here were converted in the early 19th century from paper to the making of copper sheeting. Its prime use was the protection of wooden ships from the dreaded marine worm, but legend has it that the copper orb on the dome of St Paul's Cathedral also came from here. The big mills have gone, but you can still see water streaming through the mill race, where dangling poles provide a canoe slalom course.

The Colne Valley Trail goes ahead here, but the Loop turns right up a concrete drive signed 'Bellevue Terrace' but actually a spur of Summerhouse Lane. At Barrington Drive keep ahead past houses, now on tarmac, into a shady 'tunnel' of trees. At the gate **[C]** of Parkwood Farm, pass a barrier on its left to follow a fenced path that climbs ever more steeply through the enchanted Park Wood. A bridge cuts across a stream bed, with a dingly dell down to your right, then you come out into the open with grazing land on either side. After some allotments you reach Hill End Road **[D]**, where you cross over and turn left along its pavement. Soon after passing Harefield

Care Home, turn right along Plough Lane. The main Hillingdon Trail goes ahead here, but its Northern Link sticks doggedly to the Loop a little further.

When the short lane ends you follow a route that presents eight stiles in fairly quick succession. After the first, between gates, maintain the same direction on a clear path over a field. On its far side, cross a bridge with stiles at each end and continue with a hedge on your left, a small wood on your right, and a pleasant vista of open countryside ahead. Stiles four and five, the latter with a footbridge, take you across a dip **[E]**, then continue uphill to the right of shrubs that mark an old field boundary. At the top, as well as stile number six, you cross the boundary into Hertfordshire, where the Loop remains for rest of this section and indeed the next 10 km/6.3 miles. Follow the track ahead between paddocks, where the final stile on this stretch leads on to a cinder track past **Fieldways Farm [3]**.

> The big barn of Fieldways shelters an amazing assortment of horses and carriages. Its owners, the Dent family, are also stunt co-ordinators for the entertainment industry. They are well located, being equidistant from the big studios at Pinewood, Ealing and Elstree.

Just before Harefield Road, you can safely ignore another stile **[F]** to turn right immediately past it, along a fenced permissive path behind houses. Cross a field to reach the car park of the Rose & Crown pub at Woodcock Hill **[G]** then turn left to the road. 🚌 *Infrequent non-TfL buses (none on Sundays)*

from Rickmansworth turn around here.
Cross the road and keep ahead along a fenced footpath. It leads into a dark patch of shrubbery, but you emerge into a glorious panorama, especially in late autumn, of rolling Hertfordshire fields and patches of woodland. Go slightly right downhill on a worn path to a field corner, cross a stile and continue along another permissive route, with a wood on your right. Soon you cross a shallow dip **[H]** on grass, which can get quite boggy in wet weather. As you come parallel with a lone bush out in the field, turn right up a bank **[I]** to follow a route through **Bishop's Wood Country Park [4]**, where seats are provided at frequent intervals.

Follow the broad grit path, eventually passing through a gate to continue along a wider track. Before long it dips into a shallow valley, but do not cross the bridge over its stream. Instead, turn left through a narrow gap **[J]** in a fence to follow a modest, log-bordered path beside the stream. Cross a bridge over the stream and climb a few steps, then follow the winding path, at first with a field beyond the fenced woodland edge on your left. In 65 metres the path swings right, away from the stream and fence, to continue its meandering and sometimes muddy course through a patch of mixed conifer and beech woodland.

Eventually you reach a bend **[K]** in a wider path. Turn left now, across a dip, to reach a fingerpost beside an electricity pylon, whose power lines will be watching over us for the remainder of this section. A gnarled old finger tells you that 'B'worth Heath' is somewhere

to your left, and you follow it along a cleared area beneath the power lines towards another pylon, with a road (White Hill) away to your right. The path dives into shrubbery, keeping ahead past the pylon to reach a thinly wooded grass area then the open grass of Batchworth Heath, beside a row of concrete bollards **[L]**. Keep ahead to the A404 London Road, with the welcome sight of Ye Olde Greene Man pub opposite. 🚌 *From the stop on your right in White Hill to Northwood and Ruislip; from the stop around the corner in London Road to Uxbridge (also Denham non-TfL) and to Harefield village.*

Cross the busy main road with great care then turn right and cross the two spurs of Batchworth Lane, with the forlorn former Prince of Wales pub on your right, awaiting its fate. *Away to your left is a tall stone archway, the entrance to the Moor Park estate, once the home of the Earls of Bedford but now a very fashionable golf club. The mansion [5] can be visited on certain days during the summer.*
Follow the pavement ahead a short distance, noting another coal-tax post opposite. Just before a '30' speed sign **[M]**, turn left on to a grit path. The fenceposts that you are following mark the boundary, originally between Hertfordshire and Middlesex until the latter was absorbed administratively into Greater London in 1965. At a derelict tarmac lane turn left then immediately right to resume the boundary, now a grassy and sometimes muddy track, in the same direction through woodland – beware barbed wire on your right.

Harefield West to Moor Park

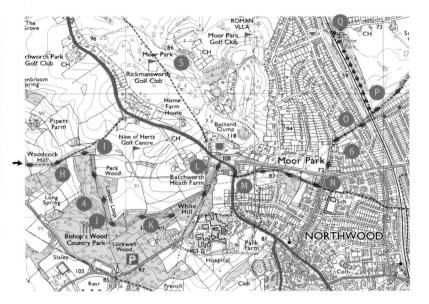

Keep ahead, ignoring a couple of rutted side-tracks, to go through a fence gap into an open area (those power lines again) and continue between high fences to reach Kewferry Road. Turn left to the junction and cross Batchworth Lane **[N]**, using the pedestrian refuge if traffic is heavy. Go past the barrier and white gates ahead to follow Bedford Road, part of the **Moor Park Conservation Area [6]** – only residents' vehicles can use the roads here but we harmless walkers are tolerated. Pass Heathside Road on your right to the point where Bedford Road bends left, then turn right on to a broad, grassy, enclosed footpath leading through a 'tunnel' of trees.

At Wolsey Road **[0]** go half left to follow a hidden path behind a tall leylandii hedge. It leads to a grass area and another road, South Approach. Keep ahead down a narrow lane (Westbury Road), under the Metropolitan Line railway, then immediately turn left along a tarmac footpath to reach a fingerpost **[P]** at the start of rough, open ground, where Section 13 ends.

To continue on to Section 14 climb half right into the open ground.

Link to Moor Park station

(0.8 km/0.5 miles). Keep ahead beside the Metropolitan Line along a grassy footpath to pass a tee on the Sandy Lodge Golf Course and continue into woodland. After passing through an old sandpit you see the golf club house away to your right, then at a tarmac area a subway leads under the railway to the ticket office of Moor Park station **[Q]** (toilets). There's a café in the parade of shops beyond the station approach.

14 Moor Park to Hatch End

6.0 km/3.7 miles plus links from Moor Park station (0.8 km/0.5 miles) and to Hatch End station (1 km/0.6 miles). You can leave the route at several bus stops as described.

Cafés at Moor Park and Hatch End. Pub at Hatch End. Toilets at Moor Park station. Best picnic opportunities at South Oxhey Playing Fields and Oxhey Woods.

Local authorities: Hertfordshire (Three Rivers District), London Borough of Harrow.

Though rather lacking notable features, this high, undulating section goes through some lovely Hertfordshire woodlands, mostly on grass and earth paths and tracks, which could be wet and muddy after heavy rain, and with three stiles.

Link from Moor Park station

(0.8 km/0.5 miles, toilets, café on far side of station approach road). From the ticket barriers **[A]** turn sharp right under the subway (signed Sandy Lodge) and climb steps to a tarmac area with a welcoming Loop information panel. Turn right along an earth path that winds through trees and an old sandpit, roughly parallel to the railway line and with Sandy Lodge Golf Course to your left. On reaching a metal barrier **[B]**, don't go through it but turn sharp left to rejoin the Loop up a narrow path.

From the barrier **[B]** climb a narrow path in a broad swathe of scrubland (an unused part of **Sandy Lodge Golf Course [1]**) beneath power lines and with trees away to each side. At the top, the path bears left, away from the power lines, to join a crossing track that leads past a tee **[C]** into the golf course proper (see page 15). Bear right across grass to join a sandy golfers' track beside a

line of trees, where the right of way is marked by a series of chunky wooden posts with yellow arrows. Continuing on grass and keeping a wary eye out for flying golf balls, cross a fairway then take a left fork through a copse. Bear slightly left, in front of another tee, to keep ahead past a bench between several tees and greens. Leave the golf course by diving through trees along a path that emerges at Sandy Lodge Lane **[D]** – watch out for traffic especially from the right as you step out.

With a good view towards Watford over Hampermill Lake in the Colne Valley, cross to the far side and turn right along the laneside path. It leads to a pair of little white fences, which mark an entrance into the Sandy Lodge estate. Cross the lane here then turn left along the opposite path, passing a filling station with a shop that sells refreshments. Follow the path around to the right, now beside the A4125 Sandy Lane, and cross it at a pedestrian refuge. Turn left on the far

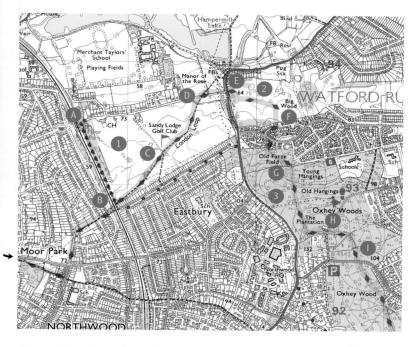

side and follow the path for 50 metres, entering Hampermill Lane.

Opposite a 'reduce speed now' sign, turn right past a low post **[E]** on to an almost hidden path in Hampermill Wood, with houses on your left. Soon turn right again along a crossing path, which winds into the fine, grassy expanse of **South Oxhey Playing Fields [2]**. Keep ahead past a seat beside Big Wood and continue in the same direction towards distant houses. Pass a Loop waymark post and another seat beside a copse then bear slightly right over a hump to reach a white barrier between oak trees at a gap in the houses. Go through a gate **[F]** and along a path to reach Ashburnham Drive, where you turn right along a parallel footway. Turn left on reaching a T-junction at Hayling Road, crossing it at a pedestrian refuge to

continue along the far side. *The bus stops here had no service at the time of writing, but non-TfL services to Bushey, Watford, Carpenders Park, Northwood and Hatch End go from Gosforth Lane, 150 metres further along Hayling Road.*

Take the first road on the right, Nairn Green, then at its end keep ahead along a narrow path into **Oxhey Woods [3]**, where there are occasional bench seats. The Loop is joined here by several local trails, and you may encounter mud and exposed roots in places. A short way in, turn left for several hundred metres to a path junction, where you bear right across a plank bridge **[G]** then climb quite steeply up a broad track, ignoring side paths. Near the top, bear right towards the sound of road traffic. Keep to the main path as it turns left at a junction,

Moor Park to Hatch End

Pinnerwood House, glimpsed over its garden pond, was the home of the author Edward Bulwer Lytton in the 1830s.

then at a broad meeting of ways turn right to the road, Oxhey Drive, beside Oxhey Wood Lodge **[H]**.

Cross the road and continue past a steel barrier along a rough path, still in Oxhey Woods. Keep ahead at two junctions then bear right past a small boggy patch and a startlingly knobbly beech tree to cross the B4542 Prestwick Road **[I]** at a pedestrian refuge. 🚌 *The same non-TfL bus services as above run*

along here; the nearest stops are 200 metres to your left. Go through a gate to resume your journey through Oxhey Woods, heading slightly leftwards, and reach a broad junction, where you bear left. *A little to your right in a clearing is a rather impractical picnic table with a seat nearby.* Follow the broad track as it bends right, drops into a sometimes soggy dip, then rises to a junction among tall trees, where you keep ahead for 20 metres to fork left on a narrow

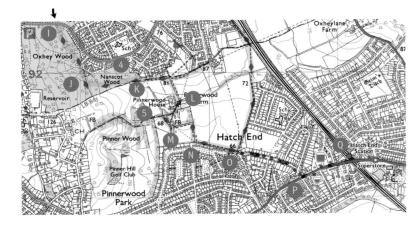

path. Descend past a huge fallen tree and cross a couple of ditches on little bridges, with houses to your left.

Continue upwards to reach a crossing path **[J]**, where you turn left and start a long descent, now in **Nanscot Wood [4]**, with Pinner Hill Golf Course over to your right. At the end, go through a kissing gate **[K]** into the horse-grazing fields of Pinnerwood Farm, thereby entering the London Borough of Harrow. Bear left along the top of the field, a hedge and houses to your left, to reach a trio of kissing gates. Now you can admire the view southwards over the farm, with St Mary's church at Harrow on the Hill prominent in the middle distance. Pass through the first gate, ignore the other two and turn right among trees to follow a hedge down the next field. You may have to negotiate a horse-trodden muddy patch beside a training paddock to go through a latched field gate **[L]** into the farmyard. Turn right on their track then immediately take a narrow, often overgrown path on your left, which winds through scrub to emerge beside the Victorian farmhouse, with its intricately moulded gable ends.

Continue along a concrete drive with, on your right, the charming, early 18th-century **Pinnerwood House [5]**, once the home of the 19th-century author Edward Bulwer-Lytton. Then on your left is the equally attractive Pinnerwood Cottage, which irrationally is larger than the house, by means of several extensions. Your second view of the house, not to be missed, comes seconds later over its pond, giving a delightful impression

of a moated farmhouse. Follow the concrete drive as it swings left then in 100 metres at a field gate **[M]** turn left along a path beside a fence. Shortly cross a stile and continue in the same direction along a field edge, with trees on your left. Turn right at the field corner and follow a hedge to cross a stile and footbridge. Go slightly rightwards across the second field, with houses to your right, and go through a kissing gate **[N]** into a vast third field. Keep ahead beside a hedge and ignore the first fingerpost to reach a second fingerpost **[O]**, where this section of the London Loop ends.

To continue on to Section 15, keep ahead a short distance to the field corner.

Loop link to Hatch End station

(1 km/0.6 miles). Turn right at the second fingerpost to cross a rather awkward stile, or you may be able to squeeze through a gap. Bear left along a path to reach Grimsdyke Road, where turn left again and follow it past Wessex Drive, Hallam Gardens and Hillview Road. Swing right at the end to reach the A410 Uxbridge Road **[P]** at Hatch End, with several cafés and food shops nearby. Turn left for 300 metres, passing a J.D. Wetherspoon's pub, The Moon and Sixpence to reach Hatch End station ⊖ **[Q]** (no toilets) on the line from Euston to Watford Junction. 🚌 From this side to Stanmore, Headstone Lane and Harrow on the Hill; from the far side to Pinner, Rayners Lane and South Harrow.

15 Hatch End to Borehamwood

13.9 km/8.6 miles plus links from Hatch End station (1 km/0.6 miles) and to Elstree & Borehamwood station (0.2 km/0.1 miles). You can leave the route at Stanmore after 8.9 km/5.5 miles or several bus stops as described.

Cafés at Hatch End, Oxhey Lane, Aldenham Reservoir, Borehamwood. Pubs at Old Redding, Aldenham Reservoir and Borehamwood. Toilets at Oxhey Lane, Stanmore station, Aldenham Reservoir and Elstree & Borehamwood station. Best picnic opportunities at Old Redding, Bentley Priory Open Space, Stanmore LIttle Common and Aldenham Reservoir.

Local authorities: London Borough of Harrow, Hertfordshire County Council (Hertsmere District).

This section has features aplenty, including the scene of W.S. Gilbert's tragic demise and the headquarters of the Royal Air Force's Fighter Command during World War II. The route is fairly level through some lovely open and wooded areas, though with a few gentle ascents and five stiles, reaching the highest point of the Loop north of the Thames.

Link from Hatch End station

(1 km/0.6 miles, no toilets). From the station exit **[A]**, walk up to the A410 Uxbridge Road and turn right for 300 metres, passing the station bus stops and J.D. Wetherspoon's pub, The Moon & Sixpence. There are also several cafés and food shops nearby. Turn right along Grimsdyke Road **[B]** and follow it for 550 metres to the end. Bear right at the junction with Wessex Drive then, after house number 98, turn right along a short path to cross a rather awkward stile (or squeeze through the gap) into a field, where you turn right to rejoin the London Loop.

At the field corner **[C]**, cross a stile into scrub woodland then turn left through a belt of trees, ignoring side turns but keeping left at a fork. Pass the top of Colburn Avenue and continue along

a path beside garden fences, with Shaftesbury Playing Fields on your right and that vast farm field now on your left. When the fences end, the path turns briefly right, past Sylvia Avenue, then left over rough scrub to a stile **[D]**. Go slightly right over a field, aiming for an electricity pylon. Almost beneath it, go through a kissing gate and along an enclosed path beside the railway fence, soon with a playing field on your left. Cross the B4542 Little Oxhey Lane then turn right on a pavement that leads to a separate footbridge **[E]** over the **West Coast Main Line [1]**, built during the mid 19th century.

The Loop follows the B4542 for 0.9 km/0.6 miles, first passing St George's Drive then along a parallel side road. *At Harrow Way, from the stops on your left to Watford, Bushey and Carpenders Park.* When the side road swings left into Romilly Drive

[F], continue up a pavement beside the B4542, with Carpenders Park Cemetery away to your left, to traffic lights **[G]** at the junction with A4008 Oxhey Lane. *On your left, just before the lights, is Carpenders Park Garden Centre which has a café and toilets.*

Go ahead over grass to cross Oxhey Lane and go through a field gate. Climb a grassy track beside a fence on scrubland that has been roughly restored from a landfill site. At the top, go through a kissing gate **[H]** to find a notice that has been amended to say 'Please follow the line of white posts as far as the cottage then continue along the track'. This is because you are entering the **Grim's Dyke Golf Course [2]**, but the notice is not quite right, so you should pay attention to our route description. You are immediately faced by a golf tee (see page 15) so be careful when following the hedge along the left-hand side of the course, ignoring another kissing gate. The line of white posts is soon reached, and you can follow them for a while. If you hear the clacking of club on ball from your left, it's because over the hedge is the golf course of Hartsbourne Country Club.

When the hedge pokes rightwards a little, follow it around to a gap on your left and go through into the golf course service area. Turn right here, past a barn – the gate on your left shows that the private land beyond is home to the **Wild Green Project [3]**, which is developing woodland for a 'food forest system' (further details from permafusion@ gmail.com). Follow the cinder access drive, known as Ass House Lane, for

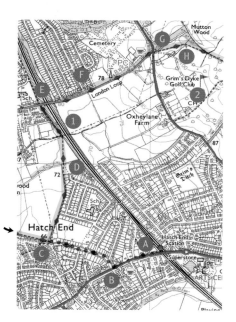

140 metres and, just before reaching a road, note on your right a low and possibly overgrown stone plinth **[I]** that bears a plaque recording **Grim's Dyke [4]**, which the Loop now follows for several hundred metres.

> There's a rather melancholy atmosphere hereabouts, and one feels that the ponds should be restored to their former very attractive condition. Yet these are the grounds of the nearby house, also called Grim's Dyke, now a hotel and once the home of the Victorian lyricist W.S. Gilbert, of Gilbert & Sullivan fame. Tragically, he drowned while trying to save the life of a young woman, so perhaps the mood is appropriate.

Turn left along a narrow path opposite the plinth into woodland, with fields to your left and the dyke to your right.

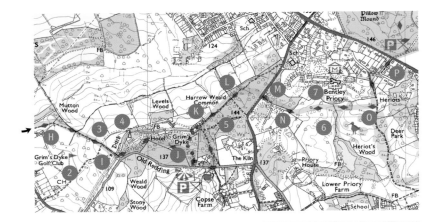

You need to watch out for exposed tree roots here. On reaching a small pond, turn right along a path over the dyke, which leads to the drive of a telecom station – its vast array of transmitters and dishes looms up to your left. Cross over and continue through banks of rhododendron along a narrow woodland path, which soon widens to pass another pond.

At the end of this pond, where some timbers to your left mark the remains of a boathouse, turn right up a bank beside a fence and along a short boardwalk over a boggy patch. Soon turn left along a broad track, with the remains of ancient digging activities all around, now on **Harrow Weald Common [5]**. The path turns right, beside the dyke again among well-spaced trees, to reach a point 50 metres before a road called Old Redding, at a nature trail post bearing the number 8 **[J]**. The Loop's official route crosses this very busy road twice, to visit a picnic site with a lovely view, and a pub, but if these are of no interest you can follow the shorter alternative route highlighted purple below and on the map.

For the alternative route, turn left at post 8 to follow the nature trail's purple arrows along a narrow woodland path and up steps to reach the tarmac drive of the Grim's Dyke Hotel. Keep ahead between low wooden posts then turn left along a wider path at post 17 – the numbering seems a little haphazard, though there is doubtless some logic to it. You reach and cross a drive, with North Lodge to your left, to rejoin the official Loop route by passing post 9 at point **[K]** below.

The Loop's official route continues across Old Redding into a car park, beyond which is a picnic field with a fine view southwards. Turn left through the car park and continue along the pavement beside the road to reach **The Case is Altered** (pub).

In 70 metres beyond the pub, cross Old Redding at a refuge then go right a little to turn left through a latch gate on to a broad track back on to Harrow Weald Common. Follow it for almost 300 metres to just before the entrance of North Lodge, where you turn right past post 9 **[K]**. You are now at the Loop's highest point north of the Thames at 158 metres/518 feet.

The Loop is now joined by the Bentley Priory Circular Walk for the next 3 km/1.9 miles. Follow the drive past a house called The Bothy, then a few more houses, where the drive ends. Keep ahead on a broad path along the woodland edge, crossing several bridges and board walks over boggy patches, and passing post 11 and a bench seat. Eventually you reach post 12, then cross two more footbridges in dips. Soon after another bench seat **[L]**, turn right along a narrow path, which immediately bears left, then left again, to reach a steep flight of steps up to the A409 Common Road opposite Glenthorne Lodge **[M]** – note the squat clocktower on an outhouse behind it. 🚌 *From the stops 100 metres to your right, this side to Bushey and Watford Junction; far side to Harrow & Wealdstone, Harrow on the Hill and South Harrow.* Cross the road to go through a field gate opposite and follow a concrete path that leads through a strip of land called The Weald, then through a kissing gate **[N]** into **Bentley Priory Open Space [6]**. No need for directions now – just follow the concrete path, which first leads to a kissing gate by a cattle-trampled muddy patch.

Just before the kissing gate, **Bentley Priory [7]** mansion, with its Italianate tower, comes into view on your left, through the fences. Now at the heart of a large, gated residential area, the mansion was the headquarters of the Royal Air Force Fighter Command during World War II and contains a fascinating museum about this wartime period, which can be reached on a 1.2-km/0.8-mile diversion from point **[P]** below.

The gate leads into a patch of woodland in a dip. Eventually the path climbs through mixed scrub and grassland to reach a Loop main sign **[O]** and information panels, accompanied by a rusting local fingerpost, at an area known as Furze Heath. Turn left along a tarmac and grit path that leads to Priory Drive, where you turn right among some very grand houses and villas. Follow it around to the left to reach A4140 The Common **[P]**. 🚌 *From the stop to your left on this side to Bushey and Watford Junction; from the stop to your right on the far side to Stanmore and Edgware.*

Cross at the refuge on your right to follow the pavement beside Warren Lane opposite. Shortly cross to the far side then turn left into a car park and keep ahead to an information panel, which tells you that you are now on **Stanmore Common [8]**. Turn right along a winding earth path, roughly parallel to the lane. It crosses a drive then takes a left fork and returns to Warren Lane, opposite the entrance to Stanmore Cricket Club. Cross diagonally left to take an earth path, which goes into woodland beside the cricket ground then between two ponds. Immediately turn right along a path above the larger pond. Halfway along, it skirts an inlet to reach a grassy area, where you turn left, back into the trees, and turn left again along a grit crossing path beside garden fences. It leads to playing fields – the home of Harrow Rugby Football Club, whose pavilion lies just ahead, but before reaching it turn right to an unmade road called Little Common. Don't follow the road but bear left along the edge of an area of grass and widely-spaced trees, then shortly turn left through a gap in the bushes to a second gap **[Q]** with a pond visible to your right. You have now arrived at **Stanmore LIttle Common [9]**.

Link with Stanmore station

(1.5 km/0.9 miles). Immediately turn right through the second gap to a larger grass area, then keep ahead to squeeze along a narrow gravel path along the right-hand side between the pond and the big house. Cross Wood Lane, turn left along the far pavement then bear right down Dennis Lane. Pass a traffic-calming chicane then, just before a barrier **[R]** in the road (another traffic-calming measure), cross over and go through a kissing gate into Stanmore Country Park. Follow a broad track to an open area then keep ahead past a Loop

fingerpost on a path that descends past post 13 into woodland. Cross a stream on a plank footbridge **[S]** at the bottom, then bear left up to a broad junction and continue ahead. After two right forks, pass an electricity sub-station to reach the top **[T]** of Kerry Avenue. Drop down to go either side of a dualled area then take the footpath ahead, which leads to A410 London Road, with Stanmore station **[U]** ⊖ (Jubilee Line) opposite (toilets).There is a small food shop but no other refreshment facilities here – the nearest cafés (no pubs) are in the town centre, 350 metres to your right. 🚌 From the stop on this side to Edgware; from the stop outside the station to Bushey, Watford Junction, Elstree & Borehamwood, Kingsbury, Hendon Central, South Harrow, Pinner and Rayners Lane.

Returning from Stanmore
station – beware it's mostly uphill, starting with 48 steps from the station platforms. Cross at the lights and keep ahead along a path to continue up Kerry Avenue. At the top **[T]**, go through a kissing gate

Hatch End to Borehamwood

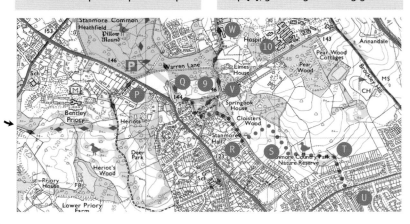

into Stanmore Country Park then bear left twice in woodland to pass an electricity substation. At an open area immediately fork left, back into trees, then keep ahead across a broad track. Drop down over a stream **[S]** then climb again, sticking to the main path. Cross another open area and through more trees to reach Dennis Lane. Cross by the barrier **[R]** and turn right up the far side to Wood Lane, where you bear left for 85 metres to the entrance of The Winter Garden – cross Wood Lane here for best visibility in both directions. Keep ahead past a bench and along a narrow gravel path between the brick house and the pond to a grassy area, where you continue ahead through a gap **[Q]** to rejoin the Loop by turning right.

The Loop continues ahead past the second gap by taking the left-most of two paths to go beside the low fence of a second pond. At a road (Wood Lane), walk ahead past the rugby club entrance **[V]**, with an imposing white house opposite, formerly the Springbok House Hospital and now the Husaini Shia Islamic Centre. Bear left (Warren Lane again) then in 200 metres and soon after The Limes, ignore The Grove ahead and turn right along an unnamed lane signed 'Public Byway No.6'. It has no pavement but has two right-hand bends, so keep left beside a straggly fragment of Stanmore Common to reach the back entrance **[W]** of the country branch of the **Royal National Orthopaedic Hospital [10]**. Go left here along a tarmac drive, and in 10 metres turn right through a small iron

gate leading on to a narrow enclosed path, which may be overgrown, with the hospital fence on your right and Stanmore Riding School on your left.

Cross a stile **[X]** as the fence turns away, then ignore a second stile and turn left down a shallow bank on to a grit farm track between grazing fields, with a good view northwards, though it includes the M1 motorway. The track descends steadily between grazing fields for 500 metres, then swings right at the bottom. Very soon, at a field gate **[Y]**, turn left on to a lesser track that climbs into an open meadow and back into Hertfordshire. The very faint path leads slightly rightwards across the grass, gradually approaching a metal fence in a line of trees, with a large blue sign on the motorway over to your right. A gap leads to a concrete drive that takes you past a fenced pumping station **[Z]** and on to the A411 Elstree Road.

Turn right under the motorway, bearing right to circuit a roundabout. Cross the A41 Watford Bypass at a refuge then bear left and right to rejoin the A411 Elstree Road. Perhaps one day we shall be able to take to the fields and avoid a roadside slog of almost 1 km/0.5 miles, but for now the Loop must follow the pavement past the Lismirrane Industrial Park and the Waterfront Business Park **[AA]**. *(non-TfL) From the stop on this side to Bushey and Watford Junction; far side to Elstree & Borehamwood.* Follow the road around bends (where the A411 becomes Watford Road), now with **Aldenham Reservoir [11]** to your left. Pass the Fishery pub-restaurant to reach a brick house **[AB]**, where

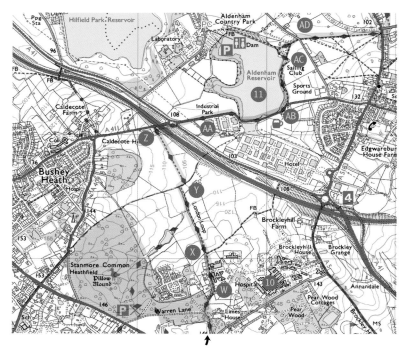

you must cross with great care at a bend for maximum visibility in both directions. Go through a gate opposite into the reservoir land then turn right along a stony permissive path that leads past Aldenham Sailing Club and its private car park to a dilapidated hut and a junction of tracks **[AC]**.

You may wish to make a 50-metre diversion leftwards here for a view of the reservoir from its dam. The reservoir and dam were hand-dug by French prisoners of war in the late 18th century to supply water to the Grand Junction Canal. Or continue along the 350-metre dam to a mini-resort with a refreshment kiosk, picnic site, toilets, pony-rides, rare breeds farm and other attractions.

The Loop goes right at the junction

along a rough drive and out to Aldenham Road **[AD]**. Cross over and take a path opposite, which goes diagonally right over a large arable field with a characteristically English view: a farm down to your left and the village of Elstree up to your right with its church spire. The path leads through a patch of scrub to a kissing gate, then continues in the same direction across open grass with some magnificent oak trees to another kissing gate **[AE]** and the busy A5183 Elstree Hill North – part of **Watling Street [12]**, the Great Roman highway from Dover through London to the north-west.

Cross over then turn left and right into the B5378 Allum Lane. 🚌 *This side to Edgware (also non-TfL to Bushey and Watford Junction); far side to Elstree & Borehamwood, High Barnet and New Barnet.* In 50 metres at the bus stop,

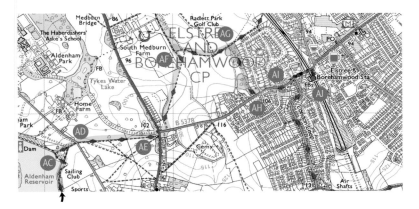

cross over and go through a kissing gate to take a path that goes slightly right across a field. Go through a line of trees and past a fence corner, then through a gate in a line of Lombardy poplars on to Radlett Park Golf Course (see page 15). Turn left along its edge, watching out for any mis-hit golf balls emanating from the tee ahead. If no golfers are preparing to play, bear right in front of the tee **[AF]** and past a line of trees, with a mound on your right. Turn right again along a grit track, beside birch trees and between a tee and a green, to a little shelter, where you keep ahead.

When the track crosses a ditch, turn left on to a path that leads into the scrub and trees of a public open space called Parkfields. At a junction **[AG]**, turn right up a bridleway to rejoin Allum Lane, where you turn left and cross over at a refuge **[AH]**. Bear left along a parallel side road, passing Nash Close at the top and Lodge Avenue at the bottom. Bear left across grass to join a tarmac path that leads back to Allum Lane and continue to a mini-roundabout at the junction **[AI]** with Deacons Hill Road.

Section 15 officially ends here and the formal route of Section 16 starts

somewhat tediously by turning right up Deacons Hill Road to the top then left along Barnet Lane. However, this involves 1.1 km/0.7 miles of road-walking and a much better informal alternative is now available, starting along the link to Elstree & Borehamwood station below and continuing in Section 16.

Link to Elstree & Borehamwood station (0.2 km/0.1 miles). Continue ahead along Allum Lane, past a filling station. Cross the railway line then turn right down steps to the forecourt of Elstree & Borehamwood station **[AJ]** (⯈Thameslink to St Pancras and Blackfriars, refreshment kiosk **[R]**, toilets). 🚌 From the station forecourt to High Barnet, New Barnet, Edgware, also (non-TfL) Radlett and St Albans. The Alfred Arms pub and several cafés can be found in Borehamwood's town centre ahead, also further along J.D. Wetherspoon's Hart & Spool. Note the local version of Hollywood's 'Walk of Fame', with stars in the pavement and panels devoted to actors associated with Elstree Studios.

16 Borehamwood to Cockfosters

17.5 km/10.9 miles plus links 0.2 km/0.1 miles from Elstree & Borehamwood station. You can leave the route at High Barnet after 12 km/7.5 miles or several bus stops as described.

Cafés at Borehamwood, Scratchwood, Barnet, Cockfosters. Pubs at Arkley, Barnet, Hadley Common, Cockfosters. Toilets at Elstree & Borehamwood station, High Barnet station, Cockfosters station. Best picnic opportunities: Woodcock Hill Village Green, Scratchwood, Moat Mount Open Space, King George's Fields, Hadley Green.

Local authorities: Hertfordshire County Council (Hertsmere District), London Borough of Barnet.

There's some wonderful countryside on this section, through woods, fields and the delightful village of Monken Hadley, but we have to cross the A1 trunk road on a tedious diversion. Much of the route is on earth paths and grass, which can be wet or muddy, and there are several fairly steep ascents but just one stile.

Link from Enfield & Borehamwood station (0.2 km/0.1 miles). From the station exit **[A]** (refreshment kiosk **[R]**, toilets) turn left to bus stop C, go up the steps and turn left for 200 metres to the foot of Deacons Hill Road **[B]**.

The official route of this section of the Loop starts by climbing Deacons Hill Road for 1 km/0.6 miles to the top **[C]** then turning left along Barnet Lane for a further 1 km/0.6 miles to point **[F]**. This very tedious stretch can now be avoided on an attractive informal alternative as described below and shown on our map by purple dots.

From the station exit **[A]** turn right to pass bus stop A then turn right again along Station Road, passing several office buildings. At the end, continue along an alleyway, which leads ahead into Coleridge Way. At its end, go left with the road for a short distance then

turn right into Auden Drive, which leads into a little square called Wordsworth Gardens. Walk left then right around the square to leave it by turning left at the next junction to a mini-roundabout **[D]**. Turn right up Vale Avenue to reach an open space called **Woodcock Hill Village Green [1]**, where you bear half right up a path through scrubland. Halfway up, pass a 'Bench of Peace' then follow the path as it swings left to the top, where there's another seat **[E]** and you can rest awhile to admire the view northwards into Hertfordshire, with the Chiltern Hills discernible on a clear day. Go left on a grassy path to pass the Armada Beacon, which has been lit on many festive occasions since the Diamond Jubilee of Queen Victoria in 1897. Continue into woodland, ignoring side paths, and later with farm fields on your left. Eventually it comes out to

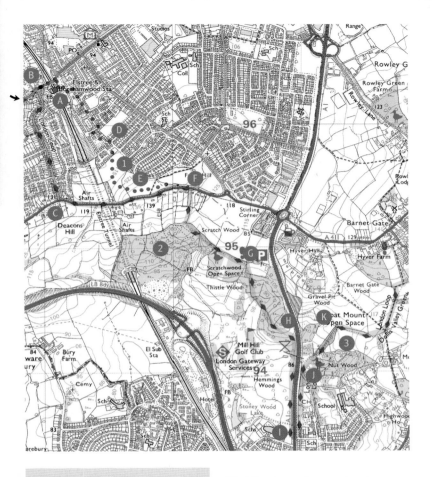

Barnet Lane opposite a house called Crosskeys **[F]**, and you must take great care crossing over.

On the far side of Barnet Lane, turn left for 15 metres then drop through a kissing gate on your right and continue down a rough path beside garden fences and across a farm track. Then, as David Sharp described it, "Go through a barrier so enormous it could keep elephants out to enter the old oak woodland of Scratchwood **[2]**, now a nature reserve, sat uneasily but defiantly between the A1 trunk road and the M1 motorway."

Mind the step and exposed roots as you enter the woods, now in the London Borough of Barnet, bearing right at first. Shortly turn left on a crossing grit path, keeping close to the woodland edge. The path dips left over a stream then climbs to an open area and continues past an elegant horseshoe of pines, with a farm field to your left. At a larger open space **[G]**, turn right down the grass, keeping close to the woodland edge. *Over to your left here, beside a car park, is a picnic area and the Django Lounge, though its opening times may not be very convenient for walkers.*

In 70 metres turn right down a rough earth path, back into the trees. It bears left over a stream then climbs and swings right to reach the A1 Barnet Way **[H]**. Sadly, there is not a safe crossing here, so we must clench our fists, turn right and endure a noisy roadside plod for 1.5 km/1 mile. Soon after an entrance to the golf course, go through a subway **[I]**. 🚈 *This side for Elstree & Borehamwood; far side for Edgware.*

Coming back on the far side, in 500 metres turn right into the car park **[J]** of **Moat Mount Open Space [3]**, where there are picnic tables. For the next 6 km/4 miles the Loop shares its route with the 16-km/10-mile Dollis Valley Greenwalk, which starts here and follows Dollis Brook to finish on Hampstead Heath. Benches have been thoughtfully provided at frequent intervals. At last we escape the roar of traffic, following a broad tarmac path leftwards to a junction. Turn right on a lesser earthen path into the woods, once the landscaped grounds of Moat Mount House. Climb a narrow avenue of trees for 90 metres then turn left at

a fingerpost to descend a short flight of steps with handrails. The path swings right, beside a stream, with the Moat Mount Outdoor Centre up to your left, and climbs past another fingerpost and a couple of benches to a kissing gate **[K]**.

Turn right, following a fenced path between farm fields, with Mote End Farm away to your right, to another kissing gate, which leads on to a farm track. Go left with it to a seat and a third kissing gate **[L]**, where you should take to a rough earth path that runs behind a hedge on the right of and parallel with the track, down through a fourth kissing gate. A pond **[4]** on your left here is recognised as the source of Dollis Brook, which flows into the River Brent. A little way on at a junction, turn right past a post numbered 12 to another junction at post 13 **[M]**, where you keep ahead. *The path beyond here is permissive, and a little notice near the ground informs you that it will be closed on one day a year, normally February 28th. If you should happen to be here on that date and find your way barred, you will need to turn left to the top then turn right*

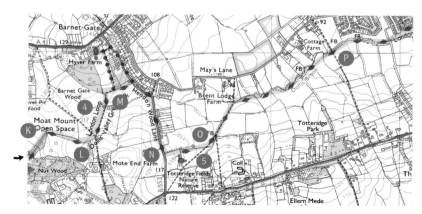

down Hendon Wood Lane, or you can reach the Gate pub in Arkley this way by turning left up the lane.

The path leads beside woodland to Hendon Wood Lane, where you cross to the far side and turn right along the pavement. A route across the fields beyond may be made available some time, but for the present the Loop must follow the lane past houses for 650 metres, around a sharp right-hand bend then climbing to the top of the hill. There you will find the entrance to Old Cholmeleians Sports Ground and immediately past that a kissing gate **[N]** on your left into **Totteridge Fields [5]**, a nature reserve managed by the London Wildlife Trust. Another permissive path drops between hedge and fence through two grazing fields, divided by another kissing gate. At the bottom go left through a third kissing gate into a sports field, with Old Cholmeleians pavilion over to your left, where refreshments may be available on match days.

Follow the lower edge of the field, and halfway along go right, across a stile and plank bridge with steps. Turn left beside hedges through two more grazing fields, with the tower of Barnet church visible in the distance ahead. In the next field, a rough path between a hedge and a fence bears right past a footbridge, which you ignore, to reach open fields again through a kissing gate **[O]**. Now you can relax and stroll through more grazing fields, via several kissing gates and plank footbridges, keeping the hedges and soon the infant Dollis Brook as well, somewhere reassuringly to your left. This rural idyll

is brought to an end by an electricity pole, where a fingerpost points you left through a gate and over the brook on a decidedly urban footbridge **[P]**.

Turn right, now with the brook on your right and the first houses of Barnet just across the field. Soon you are following a grass strip between houses and the brook. The grass broadens out and you dive into a belt of bushes on to a crossing track. Turn right then immediately left through a barrier to continue on grass, with more houses to your left in a part of Barnet called Ducks Island. Squeeze through a gap between a fallen tree and a gate then pass a concrete bridge **[Q]**, the entrance to the sports ground of East Barnet Old Grammarians. Bear left between low posts and across grass, then through a barrier to a junction of tarmac paths. Follow the path ahead, which leads over a grassy rise with the brook down to your right.

At a fingerpost beside a manhole cover, keep to the main path bearing right and swinging round to Barnet Lane. *Ignore a sign for High Barnet station – there's a shorter link later on.* Cross at the refuge **[R]** watching out especially for traffic approaching fast around the bend to your right. Turn right then left into the car park of the Barnet Table Tennis Centre. At its far end go through a hedge gap and turn left to follow a tarmac path in **Barnet Playing Fields [6]** between fenced sports pitches and open grass. At a junction, turn right up to Grasvenor Avenue **[S]**, where you turn left past Sherrards Way and continue along Fairfield Way to the junction **[T]** with the A1000 **Great**

North Road [7]. 🚌 *From the stop on your left to Elstree & Borehamwood, Edgware and (non-TfL) Potters Bar and St Albans.*

Link with High Barnet station (0.5 km/0.3 miles). Turn left up the A1000 past the bus stop to traffic lights, cross over then drop down through the station forecourt **[U]**(⊖ Northern Line, toilets). **Returning from the station,** turn left through the forecourt, cross at the lights then turn left down the A1000 to rejoin the Loop as it goes under the railway bridge.

Turn right under the Northern LIne bridge to cross at traffic lights. *The Queen's Arms pub is just a short distance ahead before crossing over, and there are cafés further on.* 🚌 *From the stop on your right to New Barnet, Oakwood, Enfield Chase, Enfield Town, Arnos Grove, Finchley Central, East Finchley, Highgate, Archway and Walthamstow Central.* Go sharp left up the right-hand side of Potters Lane, passing apartments and almshouses, with scrubland and the railway line to your left. At the top, as the road bears right, cross over to drop down some steep steps **[V]** into a field of lush grass, with the inaccessible High Barnet station away to your left. Follow the mown path to continue on a tarmac path beside a garden fence to a triangle of greenery.

Turn right along a side road, then keep ahead down Meadway to the junction **[W]** with King Edward Road. 🚌 *This side to High Barnet, far side to New*

Barnet, Oakleigh Park, Woodside Park, Arnos Grove, Bounds Green, Wood Green, Turnpike Lane. Cross over and keep ahead along Burnside Close. When it ends, take to a short tarmac footpath bending right to Bosworth Road, but before reaching it turn left through a kissing gate into **King George's Fields [8]**, bought by the council in the early 1930s to celebrate the reign of King George V. Here starts one of the finest parts of the Loop – an almost unbroken stretch of undulating Green Belt for the next 12 km/7.5 miles.

Walk ahead on a grit path, past a meadow, through two narrow belts of trees and across a stream to start a long and fairly steep climb up a grassy slope, but there's a bench halfway up and another at the top, where you can stop to admire the view south towards London. Keep right at the the top, through a kissing gate **[X]** on to Hadley Green Road, then cross over and turn right along the edge of **Hadley Green [9]** itself, where there are several seats. Near here on Easter Sunday 1471 was fought the Battle of Barnet, one of the most decisive engagements of the Wars of the Roses, when the Yorkists defeated the Lancastrians, Warwick the Kingmaker was slain and his cause lost in the mist. *Barnet's High Street, with several pubs and cafés, is just 200 metres leftwards, past a pond.* 🚌 *The bus station, behind The Spires shopping mall, lies 300 metres further on and has services in all directions.*

You are now in the delightful village of **Monken Hadley [10]**, where almost every building is of historical or architectural interest. The first

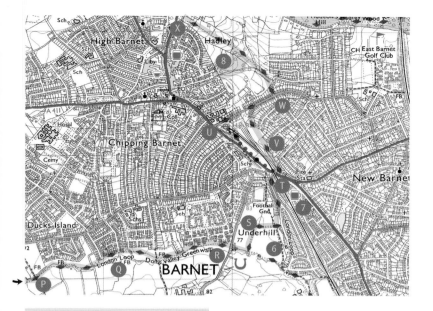

big house you pass, the red-brick Hadley House, is the former manor house, with a charming bell turret on its stable block. Then come some 18th-century cottages, one of them Livingstone Cottage, where the famous Scottish missionary and explorer, Dr David Livingstone, lived briefly in the 1850s on returning home from his first African trip. The larger house, Grandon, was the home of Fanny Trollope, the early 19th-century novelist.

The green comes to an end and the Loop bends right along Hadley Common Road, past Wilbraham's Almshouses. David Sharp again: "Sir Roger Wilbraham founded the low run of mellow brick almshouses in 1612 for 'six decayed housekeepers'. Would today's residents behind those six little doors appreciate that description, one wonders?" A delightful scene opens up

now, of Monken Hadley's 15th-century parish church of St Mary the Virgin, its side chapels and a white gateway. Another so-called Armada beacon sticks out from the top of the stair turret at the tower's nearest corner – though this one may have been set there by the monks to guide travellers over the wilds of **Enfield Chase [6]**, which stretches away to the east. Pass through the set of white gates **[Y]** – one of several similar, marking entrances into **Monken Hadley Common [11]** – beside the red-brick hulk of Hadley Lodge (with belltower and weather vane). Keep ahead along a grit path beside a road called Hadley Common, passing Camlet Way, where seats beside the cricket pitch may provide an opportunity to picnic while watching a match, but the Loop continues past more grand houses along the right-hand side of the road.

Borehamwood to Cockfosters

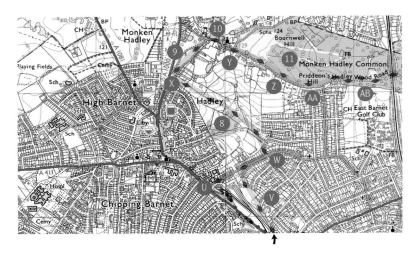

Ahead now and stretching all the way to Cockfosters is a long and narrow woodland, part of the common but known locally as Hadley Woods. In 500 metres, look out for a brick archway **[Z]** (another entrance into King George's Fields), set back to your right just before the gate shared by houses called Parkside and Bonneys. Here you cross the road and plunge into the woods, then in 15 metres at a waymark post bear right along a rough earthen path, where you must watch out for some badly exposed roots. It meanders along the woodland edge, roughly parallel with the road, to keep ahead at a crossing path. *You can make a small diversion rightwards here to another white gate at a road called The Crescent, where an appropriately eccentric red-brick house called Monkenhurst was once the home of comedian Spike Milligan.*

Continue along the woodland path, still parallel with the road, for another 150 metres to reach a Loop waymark post, where you fork left on to the road, opposite a third white gate at the top

of Hadley Road **[AA]**, into which most of the traffic turns. *The Hadley Hotel is 250 metres down Hadley Road.* The Loop continues down what is now a quiet lane, Bakers Hill, under a height restrictor, to a modest car park at the the bottom. Keep ahead past a Loop main sign **[AB]** and a barrier. The lane rises past bollards over the **East Coast main line [12]** from Kings Cross to Newcastle and Edinburgh. *Though not a formal Loop link, a path to your right just before the bridge runs beside the railway for 1 km/0.7 miles to New Barnet station* 🚆 *(no toilets), where there are several pubs and cafés.*

Ignoring steps ahead, bear right down the tarmac lane, here called Hadley Wood Road but now just a bridleway, into an 'enchanted forest' of oak and beech trees. They were planted on what were once the fields of Folly Farm, which was a popular local resort, with a funfair between the world wars. The way deteriorates into a grit track along the woodland edge and reaches a fingerpost marking the start of the Pymmes Brook Trail, which sets off to the right on a

Borehamwood to Cockfosters

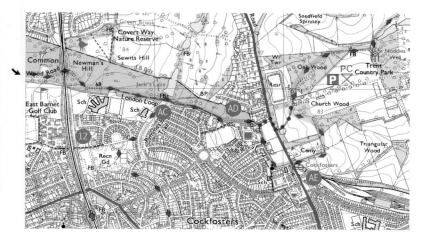

16-km/10-mile route to join the River Lea at Edmonton. The Loop continues across a pompous little four-pillared bridge **[AC]** over Monken Mead Brook. *Just beyond, it's worth making a very short diversion leftwards, over a plank footbridge and up some rather steep steps, for a surprise view along Beech Hill Lake [8], known locally as Jack's Lake, which is completely hidden from the bridleway.*

The track rises up the woodland edge, with houses through the trees on your right, to meet a long garden fence. At its end, do not join the road but bear left to continue briefly on a path in the trees, before coming out to join Games Road. Pass through another white gate **[AD]**, which takes you out of Monken Hadley Common and past an office building to the Cock Inn on Chalk Lane. The official Loop route diverts here to pass through Cockfosters station, but if you are continuing on today you can avoid this by following a more direct route into Trent Park highlighted purple below and by purple dots on our map.

Keep ahead along Chalk Lane to the A111 Cockfosters Road, turn right then cross at the refuge. Turn right then very shortly left into Trent Park and follow the drive to rejoin the official Loop route at point **[B]** in Section 17.

The official route turns right past the pub then immediately forks left past Verwood Drive and Cockfosters Bowling Club. Swing left with the road beside Christ Church to pass Christ Church House *(the church hall, which has a café open Tuesdays to Fridays 9 am to 4 pm)* to the A111 Cockfosters Road, where Cockfosters station **[AE]** ⊖ (Piccadilly Line) lies almost opposite, reached through a subway to your right. There are toilets in the station concourse and more cafés nearby in the town centre. *This side to Potters Bar (non-TfL); far side to Southgate, Arnos Grove, Bounds Green.*

To continue on to Section 17, go through the subway into the station concourse.

14 km/8.7 miles plus link to Enfield Lock Station (0.4 km/0.2 miles). You can leave the route at Gordon Hill after 9.9 km/6.2 miles, Turkey Street after 12.7 km/7.9 miles or several bus stops as described.

Cafés at Cockfosters, Trent Park and Forty Hall. Pubs at Botany Bay, The Ridgeway, Clay Hill, Enfield Wash and Enfield Lock. Toilets at Cockfosters station, Trent Park and Forty Hall. Best picnic opportunities: Trent Park, Hilly Fields Park and Turkey Street.

Local authority: London Borough of Enfield.

You are immediately in Trent Park, a fine stretch of open country in ancient Enfield Chase. Most of the rest of this section is on level ground, but you must climb over one high ridge. The paths are mostly well surfaced, shared with cyclists, but there are some rough paths, which may be muddy, a couple of stiles and two stepped footbridges. The route passes eerie Camlet Moat and goes close to Forty Hall, one of Enfield's leading attractions.

> There are toilets and a weekday café in the concourse of Cockfosters Station. More cafés and food shops are nearby.

From the ticket barriers of Cockfosters station **[A]**, ignoring the subway ahead, use the right-hand steps up to Cockfosters Road, where the bus stops are located. Turn right past the car park entrance, then immediately turn right along a footpath beside the car park and through a metal gate on to a broad 'green lane' beside Trent Park Cemetery. You come to a meadow, now in **Trent Park [1]**, and the Loop follows a winding route through fields and woods inside the park for the next 2.7 km/1.7 miles.

Continue through a line of trees into another field, turn left at a path junction, through another line of trees then across a third field to enter Church Wood. The path swings right to a junction, where you turn left, sticking to the main path, and cross a plank bridge over a muddy stream to reach a steeply sloping field. Keep to its right-hand side, with the park's Front Lodge away to your left, then, ignoring a path to your right, keep ahead through a gap in a low, green fence beside a drive serving the main car park. Turn right, keeping right, towards an obelisk **[B]** the smaller of two dedicated to the memory of various Dukes and Duchesses of Kent.

> The alternative route from Section 16 joins the main route here.

Fork right past a barrier to a fingerpost and park map at the start of an avenue of lime trees. The shrieks and groans from your right emanate from **Go Ape [2]**, an adventure course high in the trees, but the Loop goes left, past toilets. Turn right on the drive, between the park café and a car park, then just

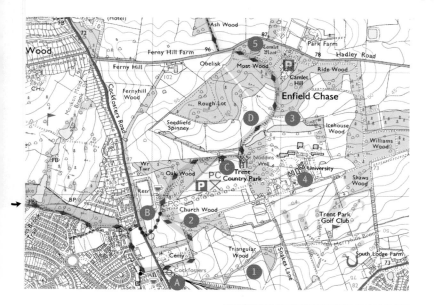

past the café turn left between low posts to find another park map beside a tall oak tree. Follow a path that immediately swings right past a Loop information panel to drop through Oak Wood.

Eventually cross a stream, with the slightly derogatory name Leeging Beech Gutter, which was dammed to form the lake you will soon pass. Keep ahead at the foot of a sloping field to a junction [C], where you dip left. The fields up to your left here are part of Ferny Hill Farm, part of the park estate. The Loop now follows a broad, firm path through grass and scattered trees, with the lake to your right, and plenty of seats. At the end of this open area you pass one fingerpost to reach a triangular junction [D] with another fingerpost and a park map. *A 250-metre diversion can be made by going ahead here to the park's delightful Japanese Water Garden [3], with a brief glimpse of the mansion up to your right.*

The Victorian mansion [4] was largely rebuilt in the 1920s for Sir Philip Sassoon. After his death in 1939. It was immediately requisitioned for use as a centre for high-ranking prisoners of war, where listening devices enabled British intelligence officers to learn about German plans including those for the V1 and V2 rockets. After World War II it became a teacher training college, then the main campus of Middlesex University, with many rather unsightly annexes. There are now plans to redevelop it for residential use.

The Loop continues leftwards through trees up Camlet Hill, with more seats over to your left and a nice view across the park. Bear left at a fork, now in Moat Wood, and sure enough, at the next junction, in a fence up to your right, is a gate that takes you apprehensively into eerie (but not to be missed) **Camlet Moat [5]**.

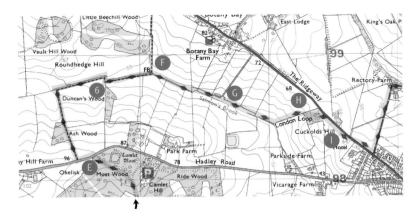

Returning to the Loop, keep on past the junction and take a right fork through a gap **[E]** to a busy road called Ferny Hill. *Before turning to the road, a 120-metre diversion leftwards is strongly recommended to see the larger obelisk [6], with a long view towards Trent Park Mansion.* You now leave Trent Park by going left along the road for 120 metres, keeping to the left-hand verge. *Ferny Hill Farm's tea room is 380 metres further along the road.* Cross over to a fingerpost, go through a kissing gate and descend a fenced footpath between fields.

It is expected that the next 4.5 km/2.8 miles of the Loop will become part of an 'Enfield Greenway' in the near future. This will result in a much-needed improvement of the surface in many places, but the route description given here may change slightly, and you should be aware that cyclists and horse-riders will then be allowed to use the route.

Turning right at the bottom, the route follows for a while the Jubilee Path, sponsored by the Enfield Preservation

Society (now the Enfield Society) to mark the Queen's Silver Jubilee in 1977. It passes through several large fields beside **Salmon's Brook [6]**, a tributary of the River Lea. There's a right-left kink into the next field, then a broad plank footbridge takes you across the brook to a path junction **[F]**, where you turn right through a gate into the third field. Now with the brook on your right, a long permissive path along a broad fenced strip takes you along the foot of more fields, through several gates and over a stile, passing a pond **[G]**. *A permissive track here leads leftwards up to the A1005 road, where turn left for the Robin Hood pub at Botany Bay, 0.7 km/0.4 miles away.*

At a fingerpost the route swings left, steeply uphill, and almost reaches the A1005 road. Just short of it turn right, through a gate **[H]**, to follow a winding path through Brooke Wood. You come to a field, with an impressive view towards The Shard and skyscrapers in the City of London, and reach a stile **[I]** leading on to the A1005, here called The Ridgeway for an obvious reason, as you will soon be descending its far side.

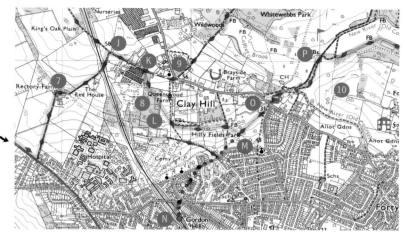

Cross the busy road with great care, then turn right on the far pavement, now on the outskirts of Enfield. 🚌 *From the stop ahead to Enfield; from the stop opposite to Potters Bar (non TfL).* Just after the hotel, turn left down the tarmac drive of Rectory Farm, preparing for the rat-tat-tat of clay pigeon shooting. The drive turns sharp right at the bottom between farm buildings and over a stream – this is our first glimpse of **Turkey Brook [7]**, another Lea tributary, and we shall have several lengthy encounters with it later. Climb gently past the rather grandiose and aptly named Red House, where bollards prevent motor vehicles going further, but walkers can continue along the tarmac and through a gate to pass under the railway line from Kings Cross to Hertford North.

The path turns sharp right at a junction **[J]**, where a huge slab of concrete could serve as a makeshift picnic table. Keep ahead on reaching quiet Strayfield Road, now in the residential district of Clay Hill.

In 170 metres, just past the back entrance of Lavender Hill Cemetery,

turn right through a gap **[K]** in a fence to follow a narrow, rather rough and often muddy footpath among trees into **Hilly Fields Park [8]**. Keep left at a junction to pass the pitch of North Enfield Cricket Club, with the pretty little Victorian yellow-brick church of **St John the Baptist [9]** on its far side. Near the far end of the pitch, by a little wooden footbridge, bear right into a field, then immediately keep left beside trees to pick up a gravel footpath on the far side. Turn right and descend to a footbridge **[L]** over Turkey Brook at a picturesque bend. Turn left after the bridge and follow the path as it winds between fields rising to your right and trees hiding the brook on your left. In 460 metres you reach a junction by another footbridge **[M]**, but don't cross it.

Link with Gordon Hill Station

(1.0 km/0.6 miles). Turn sharp right up a steep, narrow path, turning right at the top along Phipps Hatch Lane. Keep ahead, now in Cedar Road, and in 200 metres turn left along Rendlesham Road, with the station **[N]** ⇌ (no toilets) at its far end. 🚌 To

Enfield Town. **Returning from the station exit**, turn left to cross the road (Lavender Hill) and the grass area opposite, then keep ahead along Rendlesham Road. Turn right at the end along Cedar Road, passing Brigadier Hill, then keep ahead along the right-hand side of Phipps Hatch Lane. When it swings right, cross over to take the footpath opposite by a lamppost. Take the left fork down to the junction at the bottom and turn right to rejoin the Loop.

The Loop continues ahead using a new shared-use path beside Turkey Brook, with plenty of seats up to your right. It leads to a road **[O]** (Clay Hill), with the Rose & Crown pub sitting temptingly opposite. Cross the road and continue along the path for 2 km/1.3 miles beside the brook, now in **Forty Hall Park [10]**, soon swinging right into woodland to reach a junction **[P]**. *Down to your left now is, confusingly, the Old Course of the New River – more of that later.* The path twists and turns with the brook, and at one point runs parallel with a horse ride – the bridge beyond it marks the point where Cuffley Brook flows into Turkey Brook.

Plod on past a fingerpost and concrete bridge to reach a long pond, lurking behind shrubbery and beneath tall trees but popular with anglers and water birds, then a smaller one. They are probably the fishponds of Elsyng Palace, which lay near here, though almost all traces of it have disappeared. To your left now, beyond the brook, is farmland. Eventually you reach open space, with a pretty wooden latticework bridge on

your left. *Up to your right now, but out of sight, are the house, gardens and vineyard of Forty Hall [11], a 17th-century manor house, and you can reach it on a 500-metre diversion on grass up an avenue of lime trees.*

The Loop continues along the path to reach a junction **[Q]** of Greenways just before a road (Forty Hill) and if you prefer to reach Forty Hall on a firm surface you can turn right here. *This area is something of a magnet for gardeners, as the highly regarded Clockhouse Nursery lies opposite Forty Hall, while 425 metres up to you left is Myddelton House [12], whose gardens are open to the public.*

Cross Forty Hill at the lights, then turn left and immediately right on a path, passing the car park and playing field of Forty Hill Primary School. The bridge ahead is known as Maidens Bridge (Maidens Brook being an old name for Turkey Brook), and popular legend has Sir Walter Raleigh gallantly laying down his cloak over a puddle here for the benefit of Good Queen Bess. The path soon makes a little jump over a grassy embankment between fences where, in a culvert below, the **New River [13]** flows as it drops down to make way for Turkey Brook.

The Loop continues ahead through scrubland to reach the frantic, dual carriageway A10 Great Cambridge Road **[R]**, part of the Roman Ermine Street from London to Lincoln. Mercifully it can be crossed on a footbridge with about 30 steps on each side, but the bridge is due to be replaced in the near future by light-controlled surface crossings. 🚌
From stops 250 metres to your right:

this side to Waltham Cross (non-TfL); far side to Enfield and Turnpike Lane.
On the far side of the bridge, turn sharp left then immediately right on a tarmac footpath beside Enfield Cemetery. The rather sinister-looking building down to your left is a National Grid 'AGI' (Above Ground Installation).

On reaching the end of a lane (Grenville Cottages) beside a back entrance into the cemetery, keep ahead under a railway line, then shortly turn left into Winnington Road to reach Turkey Street, where the Loop turns right. *Turkey Street station [S] ⊖ lies to your left (no toilets, 30 steps up to the platforms). A footpath opposite leads over Turkey brook to a little area of seats guarded by a concrete-and-pebble sculpture of what seems to be the absurd offspring of a fish and a squirrel. And if you've done that, instead of returning to the road you can turn right to follow a brookside path past houses and back to Turkey Street, where you turn left.* Ahead lies the A1010 Hertford Road **[T]**, in a district known as Enfield Wash. Just before reaching it, turn right over the zebra crossing. *If you are in need of refreshment stay on this side to the main road and turn left, to find the Sun*

& Woolpack and Prince Albert pubs. 🚌 *From this side to Enfield Lock and Waltham Cross; far side to Enfield, Seven Sisters, Oakwood and Manor House.*

Having turned right in Hertford Road, immediately cross over it with care at the pedestrian refuge, then turn right on the far side and in 60 metres turn left along St Stephens Road. Almost immediately after it turns right, the Loop goes left past a barrier and along a tarmac footpath to rejoin Turkey Brook through **Albany Park [14]**. Cross the footbridge ahead (32 steps on each side) over the railway line to Stansted Airport and Cambridge, with Enfield Lock Station to your left. Section 17 of the London Loop ends on its far side, at the bridge **[U]** over Turkey Brook.

To continue on to Section 18, turn right beside the brook.

Link to Enfield Lock station
(350 metres). Keep ahead along Bradley Road to its end, then turn left in Ordnance Road to Enfield Lock station **[V]** ⇌ (no toilets). The Railway pub is next to the station. 🚌 From the stop this side to Enfield Town, Enfield Chase and Oakwood.

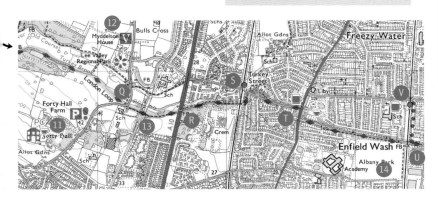

18 Enfield Lock to Chingford

7.3 km/4.5 miles plus links from Enfield Lock station (0.4 km/0.2 miles) and to Chingford station 0.3 km/0.2 miles. You can leave the route at several bus stops as described.

Cafés at Sewardstone Road and Chingford. Pub at Chingford. Toilets at Chingford station. Best picnic opportunities: Swan & Pike Pool and Sewardstone Marsh.

Local authorities: London Boroughs of Enfield and Waltham Forest, Essex County Council (Epping Forest District).

The route very soon reaches the lock itself, then follows channels of the River Lea before climbing into the rolling Sewardstone Hills and across Epping Forest to Chingford Plain. It passes the Scouts' national headquarters and there are extensive views over the vast Lea Valley reservoirs. Much of the route is on level paths but there are some long, steady climbs and short but steep descents on rough earth paths, which can be muddy at times.

Link from Enfield Lock station (0.4 km/0.2 miles). From the station platforms **[A]** turn right (over the level crossing if you came from the London direction) to pass the Railway Inn then turn right again along Bradley Road. At the end turn left before the bridge **[B]** over Turkey Brook to rejoin the Loop. There's a refreshment kiosk at the station (but no toilets) and food shops nearby.

Follow the shared use path beside Turkey Brook, which is confined here between steel and concrete walls, though there has been an attempt at prettification by making it meander through greenery. Cross Newbury Avenue and keep ahead along the path, where a ramp provides access for maintenance work. Soon bear right a little on a ramped bridge **[C]** over the A1055 Mollison Avenue. We say goodbye at last to Turkey Brook, which

now turns away to join the Small River Lea. Way ahead now you can see the Sewardstone Hills, into which the Loop will soon be climbing.

The path continues between houses and greenery, with high pylons carrying a power line to the right. For a while the Loop is accompanied by the Enfield Lock Heritage Trail, marked by brown and cream discs, then you cross Navigation Road to reach **Enfield Lock [1]** itself, flanked by the former lock-keeper's cottage. After passing the lock, the Loop briefly joins the Lea Valley Walk by turning right along the towpath of the **Lee Navigation [2]**.

For centuries people have argued about how to spell the name of this important river, and it took the toss of a coin to reach an agreement – natural manifestations such as the river itself, its valley and its riverside

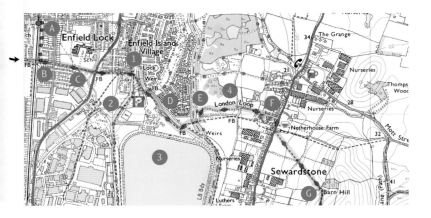

would be Lea, while Lee would be used by artificial ones such as the navigation and the regional park.

In 130 metres you reach a little pond called Swan and Pike Pool, where indeed there are usually mute swans, and perhaps a pair of mallards or coots, but the pike have disappeared. Opposite is a depot of the Canals & Rivers Trust, successors to British Waterways with its dry dock for boat repairs. Turn left through a small car park, then at its exit turn right along a curving path behind shrubbery, past a gate into a Thames Water depot. Keep ahead along a gravel path beside a channel of the Lea, which may be completely overgrown by foliage and water-lilies. Pass one bridge (where the cycle route goes left) then cross another **[D]**, slightly offset, over a channel that feeds the vast **King George's Reservoir [3]**, hidden behind a high embankment on your right.

The path continues beside a high fence to cross two more bridges – the first an older, concrete one leftwards over the Lea, then ahead on a fancy modern steel construction known as Cattlegate Footbridge **[E]** over the Horsemill

Stream. It marks the boundary with Essex, and the Loop stays in this county for the next 5.3 km/3.3 miles. Pass a barrier and swing left into **Sewardstone Marsh Nature Reserve [4]**, shortly reaching a triangular junction, where you turn right and continue along the path for 440 metres. Just over halfway you pass a little picnic area then cross a small drainage ditch between fences. The path leads into a road called Godwin Close and you follow it up to the A112 Sewardstone Road **[F]**, where a long black barn opposite contains the Netherhouse Café. *An infrequent non-TfL bus service runs along this road (not Sundays): this side for Waltham Abbey and Harlow, far side for Chingford.*

Turn right along the pavement for 100 metres to Sewardstone Close then cross over with care towards a field gate and take the stile on its right. Go half left across a grassy field, where you re-cross the Greenwich Meridian. The field is sometimes used for events and you may need to go through gaps in temporary fencing. At the far corner go through a gap to a junction of cinder tracks. Take the right-hand one, which climbs steadily up Barn Hill into those Sewardstone Hills at last. The track swings right, then climbs further up to the trees, but soon after it bends left, turn right over a stile. Through a narrow belt of trees, the path crosses another stile and keeps climbing, with the hilltop trees to its left. A third stile **[G]** takes you across wooden beams to that cinder track.

Continuing along the Loop, take the rather awkward stile opposite – there's a gap on its left but it may be covered by brambles. A worn path leads three-quarters right, through a field and over the brow of the hill, with the roof of a house visible to your right. Keep 40 metres right of an electricity pole

to find a gap in a hedge and cross a stile – and here's that cinder track again! Keep ahead into trees then turn left on a crossing path, parallel with a road (Daws Hill). This rather boggy land is Sewardstone Green, an outlying parcel of Epping Forest. On reaching a metalled farm track, turn right to Bury Road, then go left to the entrance **[H]** of Carrolls Farm.

You now have to cross over and turn left to follow this fairly busy road with great care – it has no pavement so read the Highway Code's advice on page 15. There's a verge of sorts but it is not continuous. In 400 metres turn right along the drive of **Gilwell Park [5]**,

the Scout Association's national headquarters, using its grass verge when vehicles approach. This former farm was donated to the Scout Association in 1919 as a campsite and training centre – it has often been the location of major national and international gatherings, and now has a conference centre. On reaching a junction, beside a gateway made of tree trunks, turn left then very soon, when the drive turns right into the Activities Centre, keep ahead past a barrier along a bridleway, which is known as Gilwell Lane. It can get very muddy in places, but they can be avoided on a parallel footpath on your left.

Keep right at a fork then, soon after the track starts to descend, ignore the first path to the left and in 50 metres turn left at the next one, with a waymark post. The path climbs at first to another waymark post then descends quite steeply – take care as it can be slippery when wet. At the bottom you join a track, which swings right to a five-way junction **[I]**. Turn right then fork left over a little stream and climb the main track among sparse trees to enter The Hawk Wood at the top, on the fringe of **Epping Forest [6]**.

> At 19 km/12 miles long and 4 km/ 2.5 miles wide, this great wedge of woodland provides recreation for those in London and Essex. Another royal hunting forest, it was threatened with enclosure and disposal for building land in the early 19th century, but intensive opposition from local people resulted in its eventual acquisition by the City of London in 1878.

Turn left on a crossing track **[J]** and follow it for 0.8 km/0.5 miles, along the Greater London boundary now, to reach Bury Road **[K]** again. Cross with care and keep ahead on a path into trees then immediately turn right on a horse ride. Continue past a barrier, with Jubilee Retreat over the road, the home of Orion Harriers Running Club. On reaching the open fields of Chingford Plain, turn right past a barrier then immediately left to follow a gravel path. And if you thought you'd left those great black City information boards on the far side of London, here's another – and there'll be more! Turn right to cross a car park back to Bury Road once more (beware traffic entering and leaving the car park). Turn left along the pavement to the Tee House café so named to ensure that you realise it is connected with the golf club!

Section 18 of the Loop finishes in Bury Road at lamppost number 3 **[L]**, just past the café.

To continue on to Section 19, turn left at the lamppost.

> **Link to Chingford bus and train stations** (0.3 km/0.2 miles). Cross Bury Road towards the golf course access drive then turn left on the far side to the junction with the A1069 Ranger's Road. Bear right up Station Road past Forest Approach then cross over at the pedestrian refuge and turn right. The Station House pub lies ahead on the right, and there are cafés a little further up. There are toilets and a refreshment kiosk in the train station **[M]** ⊖.

19 Chingford to Chigwell

6.2 km/3.9 miles plus links from Chingford station (0.3 km/0.2 miles) and to Chigwell station (0.4 km/0.2 miles). You can leave the route at several bus stops as described.

Cafés at Chingford, Ranger's Road, Epping New Road and Chigwell. Pubs at Ranger's Road, Epping New Road and Chigwell. Toilets at Chingford station. Best picnic opportunities: Ranger's Road and Roding Valley Recreation Ground.

Local authorities: London Borough of Waltham Forest, Essex County Council (Epping Forest District).

Continuing through Epping Forest on footpaths or grass, the Loop climbs past ancient Queen Elizabeth's Hunting Lodge then descends through fields into the Roding Valley, otherwise the terrain is fairly level, through residential areas to a lake and a nature reserve beside the River Roding. No stiles but a high footbridge to cross. The section finishes with a rather long roadside walk up to Chigwell.

Link from Chingford train and bus stations (0.3 km/0.2 miles). From the station forecourt **[A]** (cafés nearby) turn right, cross Station Road at the pedestrian refuge then turn right on the far side past Forest Approach. Bear left into Bury Road to a barrier at the golf course entrance and cross the road to lamppost number 3 **[B]** beside the Tee House Café. Keep ahead along a footpath to rejoin the Loop.

The Loop continues through **Epping Forest [1]**, at first along a gravel path on Chingford Plain for 220 metres to reach a junction of tracks beside a waymark post. Go half right to climb a broad grass track towards the left end of a line of trees, beyond which bear left.

Over to your right, the white building in the middle is **Queen Elizabeth's Hunting Lodge [2]**,

and the larger one to the right is the Royal Forest Hotel, now a Premier Inn and Brewers Fayre pub and restaurant. Here too is a new visitor centre for Epping Forest. You will be able to reach them a little further along. Said David Sharp, "Dating from the 16th century, the hunting lodge is a rare example of a 'standing', used to view the hunting in the forest below. The building is L-shaped and the shorter wing is one great staircase of solid oak – supporting the legend that Elizabeth was in the habit of riding her horse up it."

Follow the worn path, which soon swings right to a pink granite obelisk with a working water fountain, with picnic tables nearby, then continue to the A1069 Ranger's Road **[C]** beside a white, weatherboarded house called Butler's Retreat, which contains a café, nestled among some grand old oak and

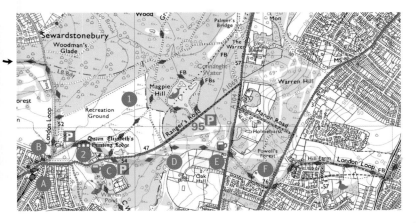

hornbeam trees. Cross the busy road to an overflow car park serving nearby Warren Pond, then turn left along an earth path running parallel with the road through scrub and trees. At a broad crossing track keep ahead across a barely distinguishable stream **[D]**, leaping over the mud and back into Essex. Immediately bear right to the foot of a broad, grassy slope where you follow a mown track up the middle. At the top, go through a wooden gate to reach the A104 Epping New Road **[E]**, with the Warren Wood pub to your right, as well as a seafood kiosk which sells hot drinks and other meals. Opposite is a row of charming Victorian cottages called Trinity Terrace, and you continue by crossing the road to go through a barrier and take a footpath to the right of the end cottage.

Keep right at a fork, then continue through trees to emerge at a cricket field. Follow the hedge ahead to reach yet another busy road, the A121 High Road in Buckhurst Hill **[F]**. 🚌 *From this side to Loughton and Debden; far side to Chingford and Walthamstow Central.* Cross over,

Queen Elizabeth's Hunting Lodge was built primarily to provide a grandstand view of hunting parties on Chingford Plain below.

using the pedestrian refuge to your left in heavy traffic, then bear left on a faint path along the grass of Roebuck Green between the High Road and a side road (North End). At one point you must come out onto North End, watching out for traffic approaching from behind. On reaching a fingerpost, turn right across North End – beware vehicles coming blind around bends. Keep ahead along a drive between houses, soon reaching a T-junction, where you turn left beside a fence leading to a footpath next to a house garage. It curves right, through a kissing gate, and becomes a gravel track, an ancient 'green lane', which descends through 'buffer land' that was acquired by the Corporation of London to prevent overdevelopment.

Go through another gate to follow the left-hand side of an open field, though you may have to walk a little further away from the hedge, depending on how the mown path has been cut. Cross a footbridge **[G]** (32 steps on each side) over the Central Line and continue to a road corner, where you turn left along Thaxted Road. When the road dips, turn right along a tarmac path, aptly called Green Walk as it follows a broad, grassy strip between houses. You soon come to a road **[H]**: Valley Road to your left, Loughton Way to your right. *From this side to Loughton and Debden; far side to Chigwell, Gants Hill and Ilford.*

Cross over, using the lights to your right if necessary, and continue along Green Walk, which after crossing Bradwell Road takes you into the **Roding Valley Recreation Ground [3]**. Keep ahead

to reach the shore of an attractive lake, with seats along the shore. Many species of water birds can be seen – we should thank the nearby M11 motorway for this, as the lake fills workings that were dug to provide it with gravel. Turn right along the lakeside path, bearing left around the head of the lake then swinging right to cross a footbridge over the **River Roding [4]**, which rises near Dunmow and flows into the Thames at Barking Creek. Immediately turn left on a rough earth (and often muddy) path beside the river, which leads into **Roding Valley Meadows [5]**, a local nature reserve.

Coming into the open at a kissing gate, fork right to meet and turn right along a gravel track, which leads to a car park serving the nature reserve. Over to your right now a vast array of curved roofs, cover a David Lloyd leisure centre, while the M11 motorway is the source of the din to your left. Turn left along the pavement along the left-hand side of the car park access road, but soon after it swings right you must cross over to continue along the far side. The buildings to your right are part of the **Guru Gobind Singh Khalsa College [6]**, formerly Buckhurst Hill County High School for Boys, now an independent, co-educational faith school. Gobind Singh (1666-1708) created the Khalsa (pure) community, to which all Sikhs now belong.

At the main road, B170 Roding Lane, turn left across the access road. It is hoped that eventually the Loop will be able to follow a better route to the north, but for now you must grit your teeth and follow a footpath up the

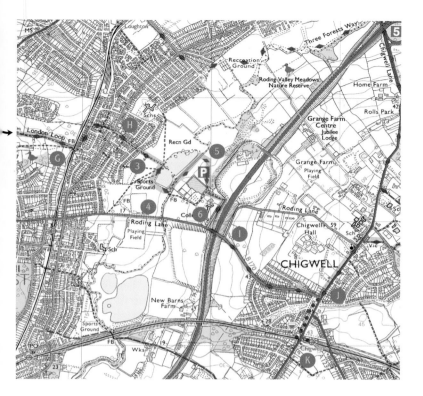

left-hand side of the road for 1 km/0.7 miles. At least there's a good view to your right across the Roding Valley towards The Shard and other London skyscrapers. After crossing the M11 motorway, at a junction **[I]**, Roding Lane shrivels up and turns left, while the road ahead becomes Chigwell Rise. It gets more residential at the top, and if you need a rest there are seats among grass and trees at Lee Grove. Section 19 ends by the mini-roundabout **[J]** at the junction where Chigwell Rise meets the A113 Chigwell High Road. 🚌 *From the stop just before the junction to Gants Hill and Ilford.*

If continuing on to Section 20 now, although the Loop officially goes left

up the far pavement, you can avoid this busy intersection by staying on the near side for 0.9 km/0.6 miles, passing Chigwell Hall, to Chigwell School, where you can cross at pedestrian lights.

Link to Chigwell station (0.4 km/0.2 miles). About 30 metres before the mini-roundabout, turn right over the pedestrian refuge, towards the 'Spanbrook' sign, then turn left and immediately right along Brook Parade, with the King William IV pub opposite. Pass shops and cafés to reach a zebra crossing at the top, with Chigwell station **[K]** 🚇 opposite.

20 Chigwell to Havering-atte-Bower

10.4 km/6.5 miles plus link from Chigwell station (0.4 km/0.2 miles). You can leave the route at Chigwell Row after 3.7 km/2.3 miles or Havering Park after 8.8 km/5.5 miles.

Cafés at Chigwell, Chigwell Hall, Hainault Forest and Havering-atte-Bower. Pub at Havering-atte-Bower. Toilets at Chigwell station and Hainault Forest. Best picnic opportunities at Chigwell Row Recreation Ground, Hainault Forest, Havering Country Park and Havering-Atte-Bower.

Local authorities: Essex County Council (Epping Forest District), London Boroughs of Redbridge and Havering.

The Loop undulates through Essex farmland to Chigwell Row then crosses Hainault Forest, past its lake, then more farmland to reach Havering Country Park. The terrain is generally fairly level, though there are a few long and steady ascents, the paths and tracks are mostly well surfaced and there are five stiles.

Link from Chigwell Station

(0.4 km/0.2 miles). Turn right out of the station **[A]** and go down Chigwell High Road, past the bus stops and crossing the A123 Hainault Road, to the mini-roundabout **[B]**, where you keep ahead to rejoin the Loop. There's a café among the shops opposite, or for something unusual you could visit Chigwell Hall – see route description.

The Loop starts Section 20 along the High Road, with the gate of **Chigwell Hall [1]** opposite. *The Victorian mansion is worth a 400-metre diversion, not only because of the attractive grounds (now a Metropolitan Police sports club) but for the café inside the hall.* Continue uphill for 0.9 km/0.6 miles, leaving behind brash, modern Chigwell, to the delightful original village **[2]** at the top of the hill.

At the traffic lights **[C]**, turn right on to a path that may be somewhat hidden

in foliage. Go through a gate then keep ahead across a paddock, where the otherwise clear path badly needs weeding in places, to Vicarage Lane. Turn right to a house called Wainscott then cross over, with special attention to vehicles coming around the bend to your right. Go through a gap and follow the path to the right, soon emerging in a field, where you turn left along its edge. As the field edge swings right, bear left through a gap then turn left along the side of a much larger field to reach a fingerpost at a five-way track junction **[D]**, where for the next 2.7 km/1.7 miles the Loop joins the Three Forests Way, a 96-km/60-mile circular route linking the forests of Epping, Hatfield and Hainault.

Turn sharp right down a track called Green Lane, past a 'no outlet' sign and a second fingerpost, with the buildings of Chigwell Row on the skyline ahead. At the bottom, by a third fingerpost at a junction, turn left up another track. In 250 metres this track gives up, and

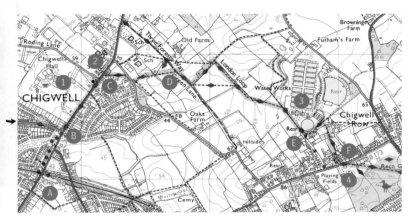

the Loop turns right beside a hedge along the left edge of a field and goes through a gap into another field. Soon after the hedge ends, at a waymark post, go half left up another field on a path that is usually kept clear through a crop. At the top, look back for a fine view of Essex farmland, with the spire of Chigwell church in the distance and Old Farm over to your right.

Go through a hedge to a crossing path, where you turn right beside the fence of **Chigwell Water Treatment Works [3]**. A drone would be useful here to see an array of twenty ponds stretching away to your left for 500 metres, but as this would attract the attention of Security you should press on beside the fence to reach a concrete drive leading to the waterworks gate. Keep ahead for 25 metres to a fingerpost **[E]** on your left, which may be hidden by foliage, and turn left along a narrow, grassy path through brambles. It may be quite overgrown at first but soon clears and broadens out beside another fence. In 150 metres look out for a broken stile on your right, cross it and follow the left-hand side of a field. You now

cross a lawn, which although part of a private garden is a right of way, to cross another stile into a paddock with horse jumps.

Go right a little to cross another broken stile (or go through the gate) and continue along a narrow path beside a garden to reach a little forecourt that serves a collection of houses at the start of Chigwell Row. Follow the gravel drive (called Chapel Lane as it serves a United Reformed Church with a charming yellow-brick Victorian front) to reach the B173 Lambourne Road **[F]**. Turn left beside the road for 75 metres then cross over to go through a gate into **Chigwell Row Recreation Ground [4]**. Bear left on a concrete path, turning left at a junction to pass between a playground and tennis courts. The field ahead is awash with dandelions in summer, backed by the handsome, Victorian All Saints Church, but sadly the Maypole pub nearby has closed. 🚌 *From the stop by the church to Hainault, Gants Hill and Ilford.*

The Loop now turns right with the concrete path, past some picnic tables,

Chigwell to Havering-atte-Bower

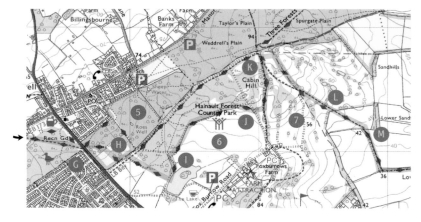

but instead of turning right again with the path, turn left across grass and over a shallow ditch to a waymark post, which marks the start of the path you now follow through Chigwell Row Wood, a local nature reserve. In 60 metres, at a triangular junction, turn left then keep ahead at two crossing paths to emerge into an open area. The path converges on to a hedge, where you go through a gate to be confronted by the very busy dual carriageway of the A1112 Romford Road **[G]**. There is no protected crossing, but you can shelter on the central reservation as you cross with very great care looking right on the first carriageway and left on the second. On the far side, turn right for 20 metres then breathe in to squeeze between posts into **Hainault Forest [5/6]**.

The Three Forests Way continues ahead here, but the Loop goes half right across grass and through a gate into a scrubby enclosure, but this has been very badly overgrown recently – see the text highlighted purple below for an alternative route if necessary. Continue diagonally across the enclosure, then at a clearing bear right

down a grassy path between trees and scrub. At the bottom go right a little through a gate **[H]**.

If the enclosure is too densely overgrown, instead of going through the gate turn right on grass, parallel with the road, for 110 metres then go through a gate on your left and cross a field diagonally right to reach the gate **[H]**.

Follow a track to a junction, turn left then immediately right past another gate to drop down a shady woodland track, now in the country park section of the forest in Redbridge borough. Ignore little signs that say 'Woodland Walk Loop' – this has nothing to do with us! Keep ahead at a crossing track then fork left to reach a lake. Turn left along the lakeside track, which soon dives into trees to reach a junction, then bear right to a fork **[I]**. The Loop now takes the left fork up a fine, sloping expanse of open grassland. *However, if by now you are in sore need of refreshment, the park café and toilets are 450 metres away.*

Take the right fork and follow the track as it twists around the lake then turns left up to the café and toilets, or at the sharp right-hand bend you can take a short cut across grass.

The Loop continues up the long, grass slope, keeping close to the trees and ignoring two gates on your left. The beacon that used to crown the summit and provided the Loop with a useful route marker has been removed, so, soon after the summit, as the ground falls away to the right, turn left at a waymark post **[J]** and hop over some logs into the trees. *There are more toilets 350 metres down to your right, at the 'farm attraction' (a children's zoo and rare breeds farm) shown on the map.* Keep ahead past a crossing track into an open area and continue across grass to reach a waymark post. You now turn left up a broken gravel track, which follows the park boundary up Cabin Hill, with **Hainault Forest Golf Course [7]** on your right. In 400 fairly steep metres, near the top, turn right through a gate **[K]** and trees to enter the golf course.

Rather than follow the official right of way over the course, an agreement has been reached with the golf club to follow a safer permissive route, mostly down a belt of trees called the Mile Plantation. A notice here says the route is marked by yellow bands on trees, which is only partly true as the bands are not always visible and in places misleading, so follow these instructions carefully and see the note on page 15. The plantation follows the boundary between the London

Boroughs of Redbridge and Havering, and the Loop spends the rest of this section in the latter.

Keep ahead across a fairway, watching out for golf balls heading your way from the left, and go left of a grove of trees, to a fingerpost, allowing golfers on the tee to your right to finish their strokes. Cross a gravel track (do not follow it) and keep ahead on a narrow path into trees (the Mile Plantation), soon turning right at a junction. In 15 metres bear left to follow an earth path that snakes down among the trees, looking out for those yellow bands. However, at one point they lead down to a boggy patch that is blocked by a fallen tree, and the path avoids this by going right a little. Cross two fairway-linking tracks, ignoring a left-pointing yellow arrow, and plunge doggedly onward along the narrow path. You come to a grassy track and continue ahead, eventually emerging beside a green. Keep to the same direction, going left of the green and past several tees to reach a waymark post **[L]** on the edge of the golf course.

Turn left along mown grass for 50 metres to find a waymark post on your right, almost hidden in the foliage, and pass the redundant stile beyond into a field. Follow a faint path going half left, heading for a broad gap between trees and a hedge, with a tall apartment block on the skyline ahead indicating that you are approaching the outskirts of Romford. On reaching the broad gap, turn right through a smaller gap **[M]**, then immediately turn left so that you are walking beside a hedge along the left-hand side of another field. Go through yet another gap into the next field and turn left, still keeping a hedge on your left. At the end keep ahead to unknit and step through a squeeze stile **[N]**, remembering to stitch it back afterwards.

Turn right along a metalled drive to pass Lower Park Farm, a motley collection of barns and brick buildings, then a smart bungalow, to reach a junction where you turn left on a well-surfaced track. Cross a little stream, the infant River Rom, which becomes the Beam lower down and joins the Thames at Dagenham. Keep on, between hedge and fence, to reach the end of a broad concrete road between fences, which seems to have forgotten what it came for – it's actually an extension of Carter Drive in Collier Row, part of Romford. The mood changes abruptly as you continue ahead along a muddy track – a reminder you that you are actually out for a walk in the country. You must pick your way carefully along the rutted surface between hedge and field for 370 metres, keeping well away from a barbed wire fence on your right, to reach, with some relief, a junction beside a green gate **[O]**. The Loop turns left here, ignoring the very obvious Pinewood Lane ahead, but bearing in mind the the infrequent bus service at Havering-atte-Bower, with none on Sundays, you may prefer to end this section here and follow the link below to Havering Park, which has frequent daily services to Romford.

Link with Havering Park bus stops (450 metres). Turn right at the junction to follow a track

beside a wooden fence, passing another green gate and a small commercial estate, to reach Clockhouse Lane **[P]** in a quiet corner of Havering Park, a district of Romford. 🚌 Buses go to Romford station from any of the three stops here – stand on the corner opposite and see which one is served first. **Returning from the bus stops**, look for the green footpath sign indicating "FP & Bridleway No.2 to Bournebridge Lane" and follow the lane northwards for 450 metres, passing bungalows, a commercial area and a green gate to reach a second green gate **[O]**, where you keep ahead to rejoin the Loop.

Follow the track, ignoring a sign for Bridleway 275, to reach a bench, where you may wish to rest a while to admire the lovely view of Park Farm and its fields, with the tall buildings of Canary Wharf and central London in the distance. In another 30 metres, turn right through a barrier into **Havering Country Park [8]**, once part of the estate of Havering Palace – yet another royal hunting park. Follow a path that runs straight ahead through woodland for 1 km/0.7 miles. It is known locally as Wellingtonia Avenue, and indeed you will soon find yourself surrounded by some magnificent examples of that species, also known as sequoia or giant redwood. You reach a junction – still ignoring that pesky Bridleway 275 – and climb ahead to reach a junction known, obviously, as Five Ways **[Q]**, with a tall fingerpost and a notice board. There are seats and picnic tables in the clearing on your right.

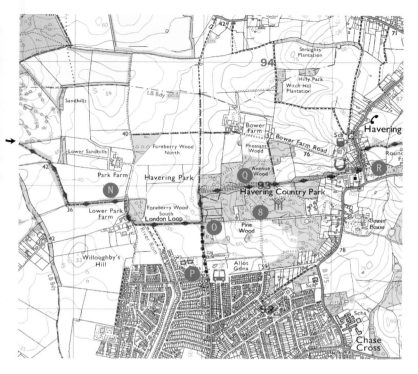

Eventually, a high fence leads you out of the woods on to a residential road (still Wellingtonia Avenue) in Havering-Atte-Bower. Here you pass Bower Hall (the village community centre) and Havering Park Riding School – look back and up to see the charming belfry and wind vane that crown its stable block. The church of St John the Evangelist is on your right, and there's a refreshment kiosk on your left, open weekends and bank holidays, really for the benefit of horse riders but walkers are welcome too. Keep ahead past the village green, which has several seats, to the B175 North Road **[R]**, where Section 20 of the Loop finishes.

The village sign in the middle of the lofty green shows a different local view on each side. It's worth going over to the far end to consider the plight of the wretches who endured the stocks and whipping post, and to admire the stunning view over Bedford Park and Romford.

To continue on to Section 21, turn left along the B175 North Road, past a bus stop and Royal Oak pub.

🚌 Infrequent services (about every 90 minutes, none on Sundays) to Romford from the stop opposite the village green; even more infrequently (once daily, not Sundays, non-TfL) from the stop to your left to Debden, Epping and Harlow.

Chigwell to Havering-atte-Bower

21 Havering-atte-Bower to Harold Wood

8.1 km/5 miles. You can leave the route at Noak Hill after 4.2 km/2.6 mile or several other bus stops as described.

Cafés at Central Park and Harold Wood. Pubs at Noak Hill and Harold Wood. Toilets at Harold Wood station. Best picnic opportunity in Pyrgo Park (on grass) and Central Park.

Local authority: London Borough of Havering.

The high, downs-like farmland at the start of this section is so lovely, you would scarcely believe you were within Greater London. 'Downs' implies 'ups', and there's certainly plenty of them, on rough tracks and grass, but no stiles. Eventually the Loop starts its final descent, dropping into the valley of the River Ingrebourne, where the route levels out on tarmac paths through suburban parks.

From the gate at the corner **[A]** of Havering-Atte-Bower's village green, walk northwards along the B175 North Street to pass the Royal Oak pub and cross over at the bend, for maximum visibility in both directions, towards a fingerpost on the far side. At first you may wonder where the path is, but it is there. Keep ahead through a green gate then squeeze between a hedge and some brick garages on to a path, joining the Havering Northern Area Circular Walk, which joins the Loop for a while. Go through a gate, keep to the right-hand side of two fields, then through another gate, looking right to see, first, the aptly named Round House Farm, with its copper crown, then the top of a white water tower. The field recesses up to the right then you go through another gate and turn sharp left to follow a grassy track down the right-hand edge of the same field. At a left-right kink, drop down to your right to cross a little wooden, gated footbridge **[B]** – it may

be overgrown and easily missed. Keep straight ahead up the rise of a field on a faint path to reach the left-hand end of a belt of trees.

Eastwards from this point, for the next 2.2 km/1.4 miles, the Loop takes a course that diverges from the right of way (marked on the map with green dashes), which follows featureless fields and is not easy to follow on the ground. So a permissive route has been created following more easily distinguishable features.

Go half left past a lone tree, on a path that is usually kept clear through the crop, to reach more trees. Ignore the track bending left and turn right beside the trees. Here you should find an elegant gatepost **[1]** – one of a pair that once graced an entry into **Pyrgo Park [2]**. They may be hidden by grass and nettles in summer, and

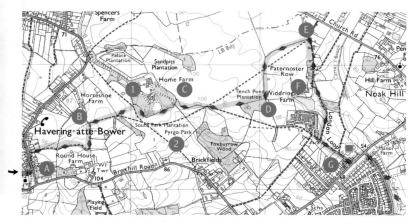

their condition is sadly deteriorating, so enjoy them while you can!

Follow the trees around to your left, looking left through a gap to see a little bell tower and wind vane atop a walled outhouse of Home Farm. On reaching a fenced enclosure, do not go immediately to the fingerpost ahead but pass through a chainwork squeeze stile – and latch it up again afterwards. Then go to the fingerpost **[C]** and turn right along the ridge, keeping the fence to your right. This is a glorious place, almost downs-like, with a view that stretches away to the south – a lovely spot for a picnic on the grass.

At the end of the ridge go through an ancient iron kissing-gate and turn right along the side of a field, now with the fence on your right – take care as the long grass hides uneven ground, and the fence may be electrified. In 60 metres, at a waymark post, the Loop strikes leftwards along a mown grass track towards the left end of some trees – the Tench Pond Plantation. The blue-grey hills away to your right are part of the North Downs in Kent, nearly 40 km/25 miles away. With an ancient

fingerpost on your right, keep ahead beside the trees then turn left with the field boundary at the corner **[D]**.

In 200 metres, just before the boundary swings left, go right to find a wooden notice and cross a simple footbridge with care, as the wooden slats may be loose, and it has been very overgrown. Turn left and keep on beside the hedge to reach a stile that leads to a lane **[E]** with the charming name of Paternoster Row – *pater noster* means 'our father' in Latin, the opening of the Lord's Prayer. Take care as you emerge, especially for vehicles coming around the blind bend to your left, as the lane has no pavement. Turn right past some houses to reach the big gates **[F]** of Widdrington Place, where the lane comes to an abrupt halt. It used to continue southward, and although a fingerpost calls it a byway, it has been downgraded to footpath status beyond this point.

Cross a stile to your left and follow the grassy track, where tarmac bubbles up occasionally to remind you of its former glory. After dropping into a dip, the track climbs to a stile on to Cummings

Hall Lane, with Lakeview Park on your right, an estate of rather plush mobile homes on the edge of a residential district called Noak Hill. Turn left down the hill to reach Noak Hill Road **[G]**, with the Bear pub on your left. 🚌 *From the stop over the road to Harold Wood, Gidea Park, Romford, Emerson Park and Hornchurch.*

The Loop now encounters a trio of suburban Harolds (Hill, Park and Wood), all taking their name from the Saxon king defeated in 1066, who owned the estate of Havering-atte-Bower. Turn left past the pub and cross the road just before a junction, then turn right along Tees Drive in Harold Hill. Cross Wincanton Road, pass a bus stop and cross Wrexham Road. Just past another bus stop **[H]**, cross over to a grass strip by the road of that name. The Loop now dives into a tree-covered gully that leads away rightwards beside **Carter's Brook [3]** – it feeds the River Ingrebourne, whose valley we now follow all the way to Rainham. The brookside path may not be to everybody's liking, as it's narrow and murky under dense foliage, so if this is not for you, stay on the grass strip beside Tees Drive.

The brookside path comes back up to the grass strip just before reaching Whitchurch Road **[I]**. Turn left to cross at the refuge, then left again over Paine's Brook (just Carter's Brook with a new name), then right on to a tarmac path. Immediately leave it by bearing right on grass to stay beside the trees. In 100 metres ignore a path that dives into the trees to your right and bear left to rejoin the tarmac path – now part of cycle route 136 heading like us

to Rainham – and continue to Dagnam Park Drive **[J]**. 🚌 *From the stop on the far side to Gidea Park, Romford and Dagenham Heathway.*

Cross over (use the zebra crossing to your right if traffic is heavy) and turn left then right through a gate into Harold Hill's **Central Park [4]**, which has seats galore. Follow the tarmac path past a BMX and skate track, then a games court, to a junction just before a bridge, but do not cross it. Go left to pass a playground, whose monstrous orange and black installations may make you wish you were a child again. There's a refreshment kiosk here. Keep on past a concrete-and-steel gymnastic installation, then guess the identities of some rusting ironwork characters of historical distinction. The broad path continues to the end of the park, bearing right a little past a small car park, to reach Petersfield Avenue **[K]**. 🚌 *From the stop 150 metres to your left on the far side to Harold Wood station.*

Cross over at the refuge and continue on a tarmac path that bears left along a grass strip, with the brook to your right again. Over St Neot's Road, pass a playground then ascend a slope leading up to your right. You must now cross one of the busiest roads around the Loop, the dual carriageway A12 Colchester Road **[L]** in Harold Park. There's no pedestrian crossing but it is possible to cross in relative safety between waves of traffic, which is regulated by lights away to the right and left. 🚌 *From the stop 100 metres to your right to Brentwood (non-TfL).* Look right as you cross the first carriageway to a path through the wooded central reservation, then look left while crossing the second carriageway. 🚌 *From the stop 160 metres to your left to Romford.*

On the far side, turn left then immediately right to follow a tarmac path through Paine's Brook Play Area, passing the Havering Dog Training Centre. Cross Church Road and turn right over the brook, now in Harold Wood. Pass the Old Brick Works Industrial Estate then in 200 metres turn left into Queens Park Road. Follow it around to the right between bollards **[M]**, continuing along the left-hand pavement. At the end, opposite Harold Wood Library, continue along Station Road, passing the King Harold pub, some cafés and a Co-op supermarket. Turn left at the end into Gubbins Lane and the end of Section 21 at Harold Wood station **[N]** *(toilets)*.

> Trains operated by TfL Rail (due to become the Elizabeth Line in 2018) go from here to Romford, Stratford, Liverpool Street, Brentwood and Shenfield. 🚌 From the stops beside the station to Romford, Upminster, Gidea Park, Hornchurch, Ockenden and Emerson Park.

To continue on to Section 22, go past the station entrance and turn left into Oak Road.

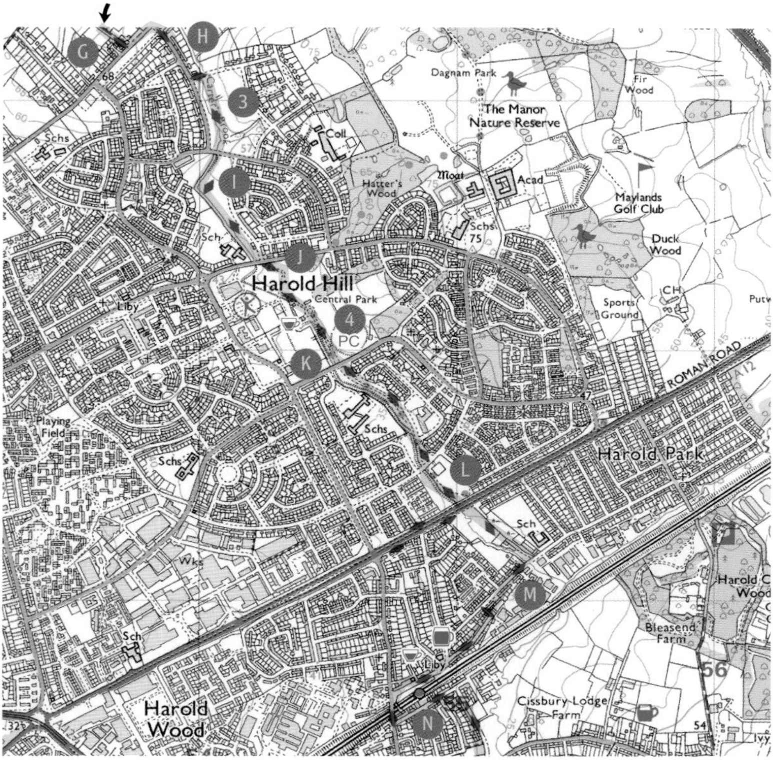

22 Harold Wood to Upminster Bridge

7 km/4.3 miles. You can leave the route at Cranham after 4 km/2.5 miles.

Cafés at Harold Wood, Harold Wood Park (seasonal) and Upminster Bridge. Pub at Upminster Bridge. Toilets at Harold Wood station, Harold Wood Park (seasonal) and Upminster Bridge (automatic). Best picnic opportunities at Harold Wood Park and Pages Wood.

Local authority: London Borough of Havering.

The Loop continues to wander gently down the Ingrebourne valley on firm terrain, through Harold Wood Park and touching the fringe of Thames Chase. You must cross the hectic Southend Arterial Road, but this is followed by a soothing patch of farmland on grass and earth paths.

From Harold Wood station exit **[A]** turn left in Gubbins Lane, cross the railway bridge then turn left along Oak Road, where there's a food shop. At Athelstan Road keep ahead, now in Fitzilian Avenue, and pass Ethelburga Road, then cross over and turn right into unmade Archibald Road, past a barrier.

A cricket match in full swing in Harold Wood Park

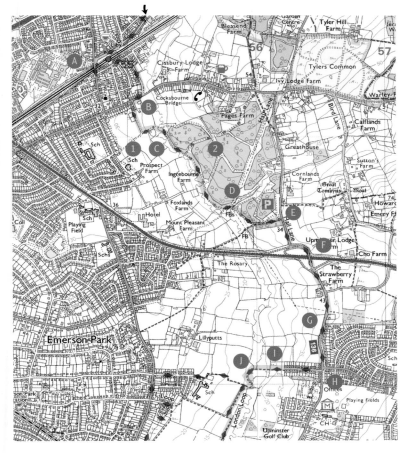

By now, the brook you followed on Section 21 has joined the Ingrebourne River, hiding behind allotments and fields on your left. At the end **[B]**, turn right into Squirrels Heath Road and cross over to continue along the far side *(use the pedestrian lights a little way ahead if traffic is heavy)*. Soon turn left into modest Brinsmead Road, which leads to a gate into **Harold Wood Park [1]**. You are faced with the blank white rear wall of Harold Wood Sports Association's pavilion, whose café and toilets are open to the public during school holidays.

Following tarmac paths, turn right, past a little herb garden, then left past a blue 'history board' and between tennis courts and a cricket pitch. At a junction, turn left past a playground to leave the park on a footbridge **[C]** over the Ingrebourne and enter **Pages Wood [2]**. It is part of Thames Chase, a superb example of co-operation between local authorities for the benefit of the community. Established in 1990 by Essex County Council, the London Boroughs of Barking & Dagenham and Havering, Brentwood Borough Council and Thurrock Council,

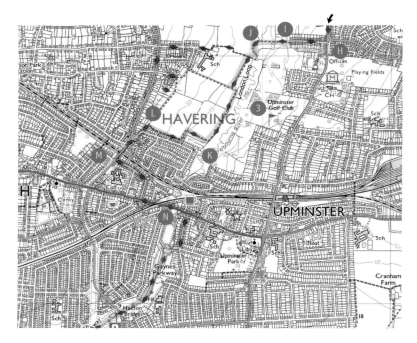

it aims to regenerate the landscape of a vast area by planting and restoring woodlands, meadows and ponds.

Turn right on a gravel track, which meanders along in company with the river, now on your right. The next 3 km/ 1.9 miles will be shared again with cycle route 136. Low posts tell you that walkers are supposed to keep left, while horse-riders keep right, but don't say what cyclists should do! There's an occasional seat, and soon after a picnic table, a junction where you go left to another junction **[D]** with a fingerpost. Turn right over a ditch, now with electricity pylons marching ahead. As the Loop turns away from the river for a while, you pass a wooden bench – a sort of stretched parrot – and climb to a cross-tracks. Take the right-hand path beside a car park then, ignoring a gate ahead, turn right up to busy Hall Lane.

Cross at a refuge **[E]** then turn right along the shared-use pavement, with the fields of Upminster Lodge Farm on either side.

The roar of traffic accompanies your approach to the A127 Southend Arterial Road. Hall Lane must give way by swinging left over a bridge **[F]**, taking the Loop with it, though some trouble has been taken to soften the blow by providing an expanse of grass and trees. After the arterial mayhem, cross a slip road to continue beside Hall Lane, pass Strawberry Hall Farm and go under those power lines. After a bus stop **[G]** (🚍 *very infrequent service to Romford*) veer left along a parallel side road then cross the two carriageways of Avon Road in Cranham. 🚍 *From the stop to your left to Upminster, Upminster Bridge and Romford.*

Turn right across Hall Lane at a refuge **[H]** and keep ahead down River Drive. The owners of the house on your left have added a touch of class to their wall, in the form of an embossed oak tree. At the bottom, squeeze through a fence **[I]**, noting a disc for the Upminster Circular Walk, which joins the Loop for a while – its logo is Upminster Windmill, which you should glimpse a little later. Continue through woodland down a rough, stony path beside a shallow ditch – beware exposed roots. The path narrows across a patch of scrub to a solid footbridge **[J]** over the Ingrebourne, then bears left on a worn path through grass to cross a simple wooden slat bridge and turn left along the side of a field. Note that some maps may still show the Loop following a route along roads to the west, which was abandoned when this shorter and better one became available.

With the river and **Upminster Golf Course [3]** over to your left, you reach a gate beside a fingerpost, cross another slat footbridge and keep ahead along a fenced path beside the playing field of Emerson Park Academy. It leads to open farmland, which may come as a surprise in this largely urban area. Turn left then right to follow the field edge, taking care as it is quite rough and uneven. Go through a gap and cross a ditch to continue in the next field, with houses in the residential district of Emerson Park over to your right, as well as the spire of St Andrew's Church in Hornchurch. Turn

right at the field corner **[K]**, climbing gently away from the Ingrebourne, then at the next corner go through bushes ahead to cross a footbridge over a ditch into another field. Turn left towards houses, then shortly right, along the field edge, with garden fences and garages 15 metres to your left.

At the top **[L]**, take a moment to look back over the gentle valley you have been walking along, before turning left along a narrow path between garden fences. It leads to a corner in Lee Gardens Avenue, where you cross to a patch of grass and turn right along the far pavement, passing Tiptree Close and Dury Falls Lane. The Loop joins a major road, Wingletye Lane, to cross a bridge **[M]** over the District Line – the green hut opposite is a social centre for people with disabilities. On the bridge, look left for a glimpse of the white stump of Upminster Windmill, 0.6 km/0.4 miles away. 🚌 *From the stop ahead to Romford.* Turn left along Minster Way, which after turning right leads to the A124 Upminster Road, where there's a café opposite.
🚌 *From the stop on this side to Upminster; far side to Emerson Park and Romford.* Cross at the pedestrian lights to Upminster Bridge station **[N]** ⊖ (District Line, no toilets), where Section 22 of the Loop ends.

To continue on to Section 23, turn left on the far side, under the railway bridge. The Windmill pub is 200 metres further along Upminster Road.

23 Upminster Bridge to Rainham

7.3 km/4.6 miles. You can leave the route at Rainham Road after 6.1 km/3.8 miles.

Cafés at Upminster Bridge, Hornchurch Country Park, Dovers Corner and Rainham. Pubs at Dovers Corner and Rainham. Toilets at Upminster Bridge (automatic), Hornchurch Country Park and Dovers Corner. Best picnic opportunities at Hacton Parkway, Hornchurch Country Park, Albyns Lake and Ingrebourne Hill.

Local authority: London Borough of Havering.

The Loop continues beside the Ingrebourne almost to its confluence with the Thames, following well-surfaced tracks through pleasant riverside parks.

There's a café and a food shop to the left of the station exit, and an automatic toilet to the right.

From the exit **[A]** of Upminster Bridge station, turn right along Upminster Road under the railway bridge, passing another café and food shop, and with the Windmill pub opposite. Cross Norfolk Road, the Ingrebourne River and Abraham Court to the next turning, Bridge Avenue **[B]**.

To visit Upminster Windmill **[1]** continue ahead (now St Mary's

The scarce emerald damselfly

Road) for 300 metres, crossing at a refuge to continue up the left-hand pavement, with the windmill behind a grass area at the top. Built in 1803, it is being restored to working order. The Old Chapel opposite, built for Protestant Dissenters in 1800, is also open to visitors at certain times.

Turn right along Bridge Avenue, a road almost exclusively comprised of bungalows. In 280 metres turn right through double gates into the entrance of **Hornchurch Football Club [2]** then bear left through the car park. Go left again past a barrier and up a tarmac path, which leads into the first of three 'parkways'. They are not out-of-town railway stations but a string of green areas beside the Ingrebourne, linked by the path you are following known here as the Ingrebourne Way. There are seats at regular intervals as well as an occasional picnic table. We are now in **Gaynes Parkway [3]**, where that cycleway 136 comes in to join the Loop again.

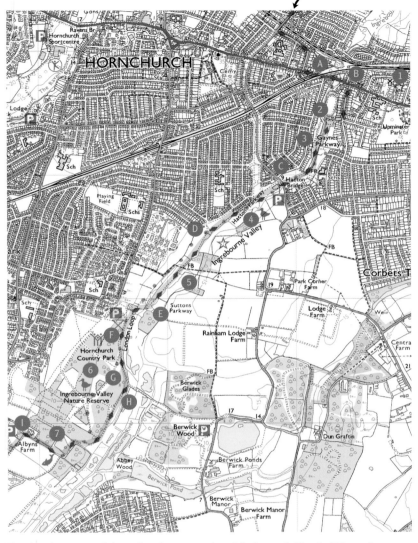

The river is on your right at first, but you soon cross it then immediately turn left so that it remains on your left for the remainder of this section. The shared-use track swings right to cross Hacton Lane **[C]** and continue past a playground to rejoin the river, now in **Hacton Parkway [4].** With houses away to your right, a tall chimney comes into view, part of the now

closed St George's Hospital. Through a fence you enter **Suttons Parkway [5]**, which has a wilder feel as part of the Ingrebourne Valley Local Nature Reserve. At a junction **[D]**, cyclists must turn right, but the Loop can continue ahead to a gate **[E]** into **Hornchurch Country Park [6]**. The river comes very close here and can overflow the path after heavy rain, in which case

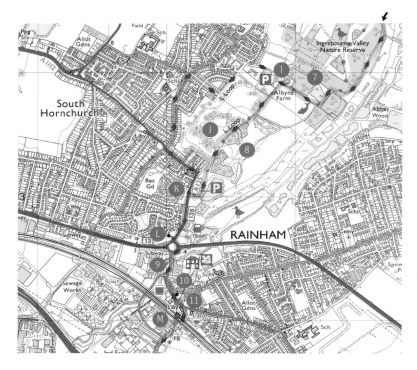

you may need to hold on to the gate and fence to get by with dry feet.

Fork left at a playground **[F]**, where there are several picnic tables, and pass the park's modern visitor centre, which has a café, shop and toilets. Keep left at a fingerpost to reach a very pleasantly located viewing bay **[G]** overlooking reed beds in the river, with more picnic tables and an identification guide to wildlife in the park. At the next fingerpost **[H]** stay on the tarmac path, indicated to Albyns Farm and Lake, as it swings right over a ridge with a concrete pillbox over to your left.

The path negotiates several bends to reach **Albyns Lake [7]**, with more picnic tables. Follow the main path around to the right – it takes you past

a high wall, which screens the area where Albyns Farm used to be, now a gated community of rather plush houses. Just a few metres further, turn left past a gate **[I]** on to a tarmac track in a field, with a hedge on your right. In 150 metres go right over a bridge, then immediately left to continue on a grit track, which rises towards **Ingrebourne Hill [8]** ahead, another landfill site that has been reclaimed for the community. Watch out for cyclists shooting across – a mountain bike course crosses ours at two points. At the brow **[J]** the buildings of Rainham appear ahead, together with a trio of giant wind turbines. Keep left at a junction to reach another lake and more picnic tables. At a junction beside mock 'runway approach lights', bear right to the A125 Rainham Road **[K]**.

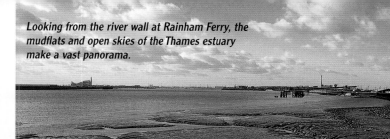

Looking from the river wall at Rainham Ferry, the mudflats and open skies of the Thames estuary make a vast panorama.

⊞ From the stop on this side for Rainham, the far side for Dagenham East and Romford .

Turn left along the shared use pavement to the Albion pub and a large traffic roundabout known as Dovers Corner **[L]**. Follow the tarmac around to the left to cross at the lights, then turn right and bear left to cross Red Bridge and say farewell to the Ingrebourne, whose waters flow on to join the Thames. Cross the service road of a vast Tesco Extra, which has a café and toilets. Its customer entrance lies ahead, but before reaching it the Loop turns right at traffic lights, then left on the far side. Cross Lamson Road then turn left and right into Bridge Road and Rainham village, passing the Bell and New Albion pubs. There's one last chance here to see a vestige of the Ingrebourne, by diving off to your right, opposite the Bell, through a paved area to a reed-filled basin where the river becomes **Rainham Creek [9]**. We hope the Loop will eventually be able to go along here and stay beside the creek all the way to the Thames.

Continue through the village past a bus stop. *⊞ To Elm Park, Dagenham East, Romford, Emerson Park and Barking.* This is Rainham Broadway, whose squat war memorial sits in front of **St Helen and St Giles [10]**, a rare example of a complete late-Norman church. Its broad, stumpy tower has little slits of Norman windows, a tiny Norman doorway can still be seen in the chancel wall, and much of the rubble stonework is literally black with age. Just past the church, on the far side, stand the iron gates of **Rainham Hall [11]**, an 18th-century Georgian house with large gardens, now a National Trust property with a café.

Keep ahead along Bridge Road, past the Phoenix pub, cross Old Station Lane and go right of the library to Rainham station **[M]**, where Section 23 of the Loop ends. Note that this station is known as Rainham (Essex) to distinguish it from another in Kent.

To continue on to Section 24, go past the station, turn right and cross the footbridge.

24 Rainham to Purfleet

7.8 km/4.8 miles plus link to Purfleet station (0.5 km/0.3 miles).

Cafés at Rainham and Rainham Marshes visitor centre. Pub at Purfleet. Toilets at Rainham station and Rainham Marshes visitor centre. Best picnic opportunity at Rainham Marshes visitor centre, but there are benches at frequent intervals along the riverside.

Local authorities: London Borough of Havering, Essex County Council (Thurrock District).

The Loop finishes as it started, beside the River Thames. After passing through a commercial district, the final stretch follows a level track between the river and Rainham Marshes Nature Reserve.

From Rainham station exit **[A]** go ahead to Ferry Lane then shortly turn right over the level crossing when clear. You are faced with a high blank wall, which abruptly severs the lane in favour of the **HS1 railway line [1]** from London to the Channel Tunnel, opened in 2007 and carrying both Eurostar trains to Paris and Brussels and Southeastern's high-speed trains to Kent. Walkers can cross over by going right, using steps or ramp – as can cyclists, because Cycle Route 136 is back with us, now joined by Cycle Route 13 from London to Norfolk. Continue on a long finger of the bridge, which points us unswervingly towards the marshes that stretch leftwards into the distance. It's tempting to think that the bridge was built specially for the Loop, but it was mainly for those who work in the nearby commercial district.

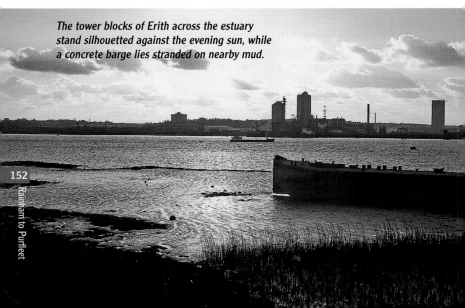

The tower blocks of Erith across the estuary stand silhouetted against the evening sun, while a concrete barge lies stranded on nearby mud.

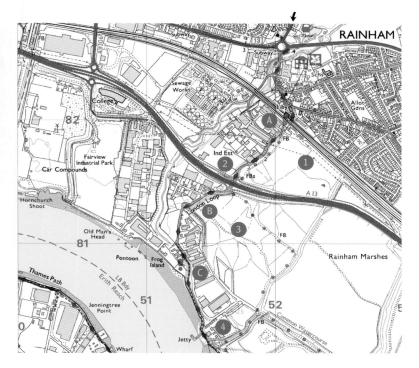

If not too misty, you should just see the Queen Elizabeth II Bridge, but there will be a closer encounter later.

Back at ground level, follow the tarmac track ahead, among grass and reeds, between a drainage ditch and Ferry Lane, busily serving the many industrial estates in this area. This track is officially known, somewhat unimaginatively, as the Rainham to Purfleet Path, where bench seats have been provided at intervals. In 350 metres cross a bridge, which seems much too substantial for the little ditch below, and continue over another bridge to reach a busy traffic roundabout. We have been trying to ignore the monstrous **Thames Gateway Bridge [2]** ahead, carrying the A13 London to Southend Road,

but can put it off no longer. Go left to cross a slip road at lights, then bear right and left to go under the bridge, through a hell's cave of concrete pillars on either side and thunderous traffic overhead.

After more lights at another slip road, go right and left up a ramp, over a bridge and through a barrier. In 20 metres the Loop parts company with the cycle routes, which continue ahead, but we can turn right along a narrow, overgrown footpath, once again between a ditch and Ferry Lane. For most of the year in a sea of wild flowers, birds and butterflies, you are now at the west end of **Rainham Marshes Nature Reserve [3]**, an all-embracing term that includes the Wennington and Aveley Marshes

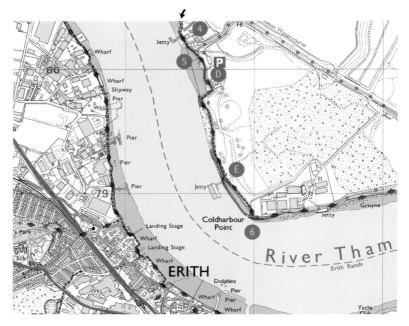

further along. Much of it was an army firing range, and unexploded ordnance continues to pop up from time to time. Vacated by the military in 2000, the area is now an immense nature reserve of the Royal Society for the Protection of Birds. In 275 metres the path swings left **[B]** to continue for another 450 metres, now in company with Coldharbour Lane. Cross the lane and keep ahead along a short but broad and grassy path between commercial buildings to cross Ferry Lane **[C]**, back again but much quieter now.

Climb a concrete ramp to your left and continue beside a fence. It has been quite overgrown along here, and if necessary you can instead turn left along Ferry Lane for 330 metres, beside warehouses, to climb a flight of steps on your right, after which the path becomes clearer. Confronting you now is a phalanx of silos guarding the **Tilda Rice factory [4]** ahead, but

you give them the slip by swerving right and crossing a bridge to join the river wall. The Thames is now in full view and you follow it all the way to Purfleet, with water birds and frequent river traffic to divert your attention. This stretch is known as the Havering Riverside Path. where bright orange panels will tell you much more than there's room for here.

A jetty here is occasionally used to bring supplies to the rice factory, then the path may be temporarily closed while lorries cross. As a pipeline dives into the river, a bizarre collection of sixteen part-sunken barges **[5]** comes into view, but no ordinary barges these. They are made of concrete, first towed across the Channel as part of the Mulberry Harbour that supported the D-Day landings of World War II. Then in 1953 they served a second duty, shoring up the estuary flood defences, but nobody wants them anymore. The cycle routes come back

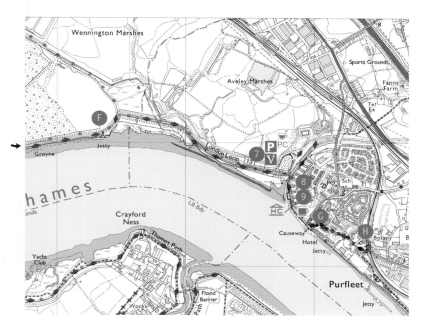

here, through a car park **[D]** on your left. Across the river now is Erith, where the Loop started its circumnavigation, with the spire of St John the Baptist church prominent. The path wanders around a marshy area, with the vast Rainham landfill and recycling centre over to the left, mercifully hidden by a tall embankment, but if the wind is from the north-east you may catch a whiff – best not to know what of! It is supplied not only by land but by sea, through a great shed that appears to be floating in mid-river.

After crossing a concrete road **[E]** that serves the shed (beware heavy lorries) you round **Coldharbour Point [6]** with London's only lighthouse, painted bright red. That long Ferry Lane used to come here, and if the ferry to Erith still operated you might have been using it to complete the Loop now, but it's still another 3.5 km/2.2 miles to

Purfleet. Ahead now and much closer is the Queen Elizabeth II Bridge (see page 22) though it's still nearly 6.2 km/4 miles away. After passing a large commercial estate you come to an area of salt marsh, where the track swings left to a gate **[F]** and a small car park, but just before the gate turn right along a path and back into Essex. It drops to another tarmac track, which you are supposed to use, but there's no view of the river down there, so walkers can follow the embankment for 1.3 km/0.8 miles, though it's a little rough and stony in places.

Across the Thames now rises the Darent Flood Barrier from Section 1 (see page 22). Down to your left, a green fence encloses the public area of the nature reserve, actually on Aveley Marshes – you have to pay to enter via the visitor centre. The rusty brown shed is a birdwatchers' hide. Eventually you reach the **visitor centre [7]**, accessed by a solidly built footbridge: the café, shop and viewing centre are on the upper level, the toilets are down the steps. Tearing yourself away from the visitor centre, you still have some work to do. Fork right on a narrower path to cross **Mar Dyke [8]**, a short and little-known Essex river that rises near Upminster – the sluices are opened daily to let the backed-up water flow into the Thames. Turn right on the far side, passing an aluminium arch, which describes half a million years of Purfleet's history. Continue beside the river wall, looking back for a distant final view of Canary Wharf and The Shard, 22 km/14 miles away.

After some houses you reach a long brick shed – Magazine Number 5, built in 1759, which once stored gunpowder but now houses the **Purfleet Heritage Museum [9]** – and a grass area with Purfleet's Millennium Beacon and coat-of-arms signpost. Bear left on a footpath leading to the Royal Hotel **[G]** on London Road, where the London Loop finishes. This is a suitable place for a celebratory pint, and you may prefer not to know that, according to a green plaque opposite, in Bram Stoker's novel 'Dracula' the bloodthirsty Count moved to Carfax House, which is thought to have been based on a house near here.

If you have now completed the London Loop, well done! You can claim a certificate by visiting Transport for London's Walking Pages at tfl.gov.uk/walking.

Non-TfL services from the stop on this side of London Road for Ockendon or Basildon; far side for Grays or Lakeside.

Link to Purfleet Station (430 metres). Turn right along London Road to a mini-roundabout and keep ahead for another 330 metres, crossing to the far side when the pavement runs out. The station **[H]** (no toilets) is on the line from Fenchurch Street to Tilbury and Southend but Oyster, Travelcards and Freedom passes are not valid so you will have to buy a ticket to Rainham. No cafés here but there's a food shop a short distance ahead past the level crossing.

Travelling from Section 24 to Section 1. Not all Loop walkers start at Erith and may still have a way to go – some may be keen enough to want to continue on to Section 1 now. Unfortunately, this is not easy as there is as yet no convenient river crossing. The most practical way is to take a train from Purfleet to West Ham, then Docklands Light Railway to Woolwich and train to Erith – this should take about an hour and a quarter. A taxi via the Queen Elizabeth II Bridge would be quicker but much more expensive.

PART THREE
USEFUL INFORMATION

The information provided in this section and in the route descriptions was valid at the time of publication but is subject to change at any time – always check with the relevant website or information number.

Transport

It will make good sense for most London Loop walkers to use London's excellent public transport system – this offers many advantages, even for motorists. For a start, there's no need to worry about finding a parking space; you won't need to get back to your car, which may not be easy when the finish of the walk is a long way from the start; you can forget about the security of your vehicle, minimise pollution and have a beer or two with no qualms.

Most Londoners will rely on pay as you go or an Oyster card for their journey, while pensioners will carry their Freedom Pass, but for visitors to London the most economical way will be to buy the approprate Travelcard for the zones you need. The Distance Calculator below tells you the zone of the main places with public transport along the route.

The mention of a station on a bus link does not necessarily mean it is within the London travel zones – you are advised to check before travelling.

Christmas Day and Boxing Day.
No services operate on Christmas Day. On Boxing Day, most bus, Tube, tram, Docklands Light Railway and London Overground services operate at a reduced frequency; some National Rail services operate at a reduced frequency but most do not operate at all.

Ticketing Information

Pay as you go. By far the easiest and most convenient way to pay for travel in London is to pay as you go. If you already have a contactless payment card or mobile device, then you're ready to go! You can use pay as you go to travel on all Transport for London (TfL) services and most National Rail services in London (not Heathrow Express services or between Hayes & Harlington and Heathrow on Heathrow Connect services). Just make sure that you touch in at the start and touch out at the finish of your journey. On buses and trams, just touch in as you board. The fare charged depends on when you travel and which service you use. Most Tube and National Rail services covering stations along the London Loop are in Zones 4, 5 or 6. The only exceptions are Ewell East, Ewell West and Purfleet, which are outside the London zones.

To check the fare before you travel, go to *www.tfl.gov.uk/fares*. For individual journey fares, you should use TfL's single fare finder: *https://tfl.gov.uk/fares-and-payments/fares/single-fare-finder*.

If you don't have a contactless payment card or device, you can get an Oyster card and put money on it to pay as you go. Get an Oyster card online *(https://oyster.tfl.gov.uk)* from an Oyster Stop (in newsagents across London) at Tube, London Overground, TfL Rail and some DLR and National Rail stations, or TfL Visitor Centres.

You can buy a Day Travelcard or a One Day Bus & Tram Pass (see below), but generally pay as you go is better value as you only pay for the journeys you make. When the total cost for all journeys reaches a pre-determined limit, a cap is applied. When you reach a cap, you won't be charged for further journeys in the same zones for the rest of the day. For further information visit *https://tfl.gov.uk/fares-and-payments/contactless/what-is-capping*.

Day Travelcards. These allow you to travel as much as you like, as often as you like for one day. You can use them on bus, Tube, tram, DLR, London Overground, TfL Rail and most National Rail services within London. You will need to check when buying whether you need an Anytime or Off-peak Travelcard. Day Travelcards can also be used on the Emirates Air Line and some river services.

One Day Bus & Tram Passes. You can buy a One Day Bus & Tram Pass from Oyster Ticket Stops (newsagents across London) or Tube stations. It gives you unlimited travel on all TfL buses and

trams. However, you may prefer to pay as you go with a contactless payment or Oyster card as you only pay for the journeys you make.

Freedom Passes. If you have a London Freedom Pass, you can use it at any time for any journey operated by TfL (buses, trains, Tube, London Overground, Docklands Light Railway, TfL Rail). You can use it on local buses that are not operated by TfL but only between 09.30 and 23.00, or any time at weekends or public holidays. It can be used on National Rail services within Greater London on Mondays to Fridays between 09.30 and 04.30 the following morning, and at any time at weekends or on public holidays. A Freedom Pass also entitles the holder to a discount on some river services and the Emirates Air Line.

Discounted or free travel. If you have a valid English National Concessionary Travel scheme bus pass, you can use this on all TfL bus and tram services. If you have a Railcard, or participate in another suitable discount scheme, you can get the discount set on an Oyster card to get reduced off-peak pay as you go travel.

Services outside Greater London. Except for Freedom Passes, the tickets described above are not accepted on most bus routes serving the London Loop outside Greater London, indicated 'non-TfL' in the route descriptions. They are also not accepted for journeys to or from Ewell East, Ewell West or Purfleet stations. For these journeys you will have to pay the appropriate excess fare.

You can get more information at *www.tfl.gov.uk/fares*.

Travel Information

Most services within Greater London are reasonably frequent, even on Saturdays and Sundays. However, especially outside Greater London, some services operate less frequently at weekends and in a few cases not at all on Sundays. You are advised to check service details in advance. Details of services and times for all London's transport services can be obtained from the TfL Journey Planner service, by phone on 0343 222 1234 or online at *https://journeyplanner.tfl.gov.uk*. For details of services outside London, contact Traveline at *www.travelinesoutheast.org.uk* or the relevant county's information line or website shown in the Useful Addresses section.

Distance Calculator

To help plan your walks, these are the main staging points (places where public transport is available) for each of the 24 official sections of the London Loop. The distances shown are to the nearest point on the main route, so you may need to add link distances. There are many intermediate bus stops, as indicated in the route descriptions. Buses within Greater London do not operate in zones – Travelcards are valid for any bus journey.

* Outside Oyster/Travelcard zones. <> To/from these stations.

Section	Zone	km	miles	Starting point/operator/principal London ⇌ stations
1	6	–	–	⇌ **Erith**. Southeastern/London Bridge, Cannon Street, Waterloo East, Charing Cross. Link + 0.4 km/0.2 miles.
	6	4.9	3.0	⇌ **Slade Green**. Southeastern/London Bridge, Cannon Street, Waterloo East, Charing Cross. Link + 1.3 km/0.8 miles.
	6	4.3	2.7	⇌ **Crayford**. Southeastern/London Bridge, Cannon Street, Waterloo East, Charing Cross. Link + 0.5 km/0.3 miles.
2	6	4.2	2.6	⇌ **Bexley**. Southeastern/London Bridge, Cannon Street, Waterloo East, Charing Cross. Link + 0.2 km/0.1 miles.
	-	3.9	2.4	🚇 **Foots Cray**. <> Sidcup.
	-	1.8	1.1	🚇 **Queen Mary's Hospital**. <> Sidcup, Chislehurst.
3	5	7.3	4.5	⇌ **Petts Wood**. Southeastern/Victoria, London Bridge, Cannon Street, Waterloo East, Charing Cross. Link + 0.7 km/0.4 miles.

Section	Zone	km	miles	Starting point/operator/principal London ⇌ stations
	-	3.0	1.9	🚌 **Crofton Road**. <> Orpington, Petts Wood, Bromley South, Hayes.
	-	1.9	1.2	🚌 **Farnborough (Kent)**. <> Orpington, Bromley South, Crystal Palace.
	-	6.3	3.9	🚌 **Keston**. <> Bromley South, Hayes.
4	6	2.0	1.3	⇌ **Hayes (Kent)**. South Eastern/London Bridge, Cannon Street, Waterloo East, Charing Cross. Link + 1.0 km/0.6 miles.
	-	5.6	3.5	🚌 **Shirley Hills Road**. <> East Croydon, Norwood Junction, Purley Oaks.
	3-6	1.1	0.7	🚋 **Coombe Lane**. <> East Croydon.
	-	2.3	1.4	🚌 **Selsdon Park Road**. <> East and West Croydon.
5	-	5.0	3.1	🚌 **Hamsey Green**. <> East and West Croydon.
	-	2.4	1.5	🚌 **Godstone Road**. <> West Croydon.
	-	3.6	2.2	🚌 **Coulsdon Road**. <> Purley Oaks, East Croydon.
6	6	4.3	2.7	⇌ **Coulsdon South**. Southern/London Bridge.
	-	1.8	1.1	🚌 **Clocktower village**. <> Coulsdon South, Wallington, Mitcham Eastfields.
	-	2.5	1.6	🚌 **The Oaks Park**. <> Purley, West Croydon.
7	6	3.3	2.1	⇌ **Banstead**. Southern/Victoria. Link + 0.5 km/ 0.3 miles. No Sunday service – see page 56.
	*	3.4	2.1	⇌ **Ewell East**. Southern/Victoria, London Bridge. Link + 1.3 km/0.8 miles.
8	*	2.2	1.3	⇌ **Ewell West**. South West/Clapham Junction, Vauxhall, Waterloo. Link + 0.4 km/0.3 miles.
	-	3.0	1.9	🚌 **Ruxley Lane**. <> Tolworth, Kingston.
	-	1.0	0.6	🚌 **Kingston Road**. <> Tolworth, Kingston.
	4	2.9	1.8	⇌ **Malden Manor**. South West/Clapham Junction, Vauxhall, Waterloo. Link + 0.4 km/0.3 miles.
		2.7	1.7	⇌ **Berrylands**. South West/Clapham Junction, Vauxhall, Waterloo.

Useful Information

Section	Zone	km	miles	Starting point/operator/principal London ⇌ stations
9	6	2.7	1.7	⇌ **Kingston**. South West/Clapham Junction, Vauxhall, Waterloo. Link + 0.6 km/0.4 miles.
	-	5.5	3.5	⇌ **Fulwell**. South West/Clapham Junction, Vauxhall, Waterloo. Link + 0.5 km/0.3 miles.
	-	4.1	2.6	🚇 **Hanworth Road**. <> Hampton, Kingston, Hounslow, Heathrow Central.
10	5/6	5.2	3.3	⊖ **Hatton Cross**. Piccadilly Line. Link + 1.0 km/0.6 miles.
	-	2.3	1.4	🚇 **Bath Road**. <> Hayes & Harlington, West Drayton, Uxbridge, Heathrow Central.
11	5	4.2	2.6	⇌ **Hayes & Harlington**. Great Western/Ealing Broadway, Paddington. Link + 0.2 km/0.1 miles.
	6	4.4	2.7	⇌ **West Drayton**. Great Western/Ealing Broadway, Paddington. Link + 0.2 km/0.1 miles.
12	6	6.5	4.0	⊖ **Uxbridge**. Piccadilly Line. Link + 0.7 km/0.4 miles.
		4.8	3.0	🚇 **South Harefield**. <> Uxbridge.
13	-	2.9	1.8	🚇 **Harefield West**. <> Uxbridge. Link + 0.2 km/0.1 miles.
	-	5.8	3.6	🚇 **Batchworth Heath**. <> Northwood, Ruislip, Uxbridge.
14	6	1.8	1.1	⊖ **Moor Park**. Metropolitan Line. Link + 0.8 km/0.5 miles.
	-	2.1	1.3	🚇 **Hayling Road, Prestwick Road** (non-TfL). <> Bushey, Watford, Carpenders Park, Northwood, Hatch End.
15	6	3.8	2.4	⊖ **Hatch End**. Willesden Junction, London Euston (also Watford Junction non-TfL). Link + 1.0 km/0.6 miles.
	-	5.0	3.1	🚇 **Common** Road <> Stanmore, Edgware, Bushey.
	5	2.4	1.5	⊖ **Stanmore**. Jubilee Line. Link + 1.5 km/0.9 miles.
	-	4.6	2.8	🚇 **Watling Street** (non-TfL). <> Bushey, Watford, Elstree & Borehamwood.

Useful Information

Section	Zone	km	miles	Starting point/operator/principal London ⇌ stations
16	6	2.0	1.2	⇌ **Elstree & Borehamwood**. Thameslink/St Pancras, Blackfriars. Link + 0.2 km/0.1 miles.
		4.5	2.8	🚌 **A1 Barnet Way**. <> Edgware, Elstree & Borehamwood.
	5	7.1	4.4	⊖ **High Barnet**. Northern Line. Link + 0.5 km/0.3 miles.
17	5	6.0	3.7	⊖ **Cockfosters**. Piccadilly Line.
	-	6.6	4.1	🚌 **The Ridgeway**. <> Enfield Chase, Enfield Town (also Potters Bar non-TfL).
	5	2.5	1.6	⇌ **Gordon Hill**. Great Northern/Finsbury Park, Moorgate. Link + 0.9 km/0.5 miles.
	-	2.8	1.8	🚌 **Great Cambridge Road**. <> Enfield Town, Enfield Chase, Turnpike Lane (also Waltham Cross non-TfL).
	6	0.7	0.4	⊖ **Turkey Street**. Seven Sisters, Liverpool Street.
18	6	1.4	0.9	⇌ **Enfield Lock**. Greater Anglia/Tottenham Hale. Liverpool Street. Link + 0.4 km/0.2 miles.
19	5	7.3	4.5	⊖ **Chingford**. Walthamstow Central, Liverpool Street. Link + 0.3 km/0.2 miles.
	-	1.9	1.2	🚌 **Buckhurst Hill**. <> Loughton, Debden, Chingford, Walthamstow Central.
20	4	4.3	2.7	⊖ **Chigwell**. Central Line. Link + 0.4 km/0.2 miles.
	-	3.4	2.1	🚌 **Chigwell Row**. <> Hainault, Gants Hill, Ilford.
	-	5.4	3.3	🚌 **Havering Park**. <> Romford.
21	-	1.5	1.0	🚌 **Havering-atte-Bower**. <> Romford.
	-	5.7	3.6	🚌 **Noak Hill**. <> Harold Wood, Gidea Park, Romford, Emerson Park, Hornchurch.
22	6	3.9	2.4	⇌ **Harold Wood**. TfL Rail/Liverpool Street. (From 2019 this will become the Elizabeth Line through central London to Heathrow and Reading.)
	-	4.0	2.5	🚌 **Cranham**. <> Upminster, Upminster Bridge, Romford.
23	6	2.9	1.8	⊖ **Upminster Bridge**. District Line.

Section	Zone	km	miles	Starting point/operator/principal London 🚉 stations
24	6	7.3	4.6	🚉 **Rainham (Essex)**. C2C/Barking, West Ham, Fenchurch Street. Note there's another Rainham in Kent.
	*	7.8	4.8	🚉 **Purfleet**. C2C/Barking, West Ham, Fenchurch Street. Link + 0.5 km/0.3 miles.

USEFUL ADDRESSES

Where no email address is shown, use the online contact form on the website.

Buckinghamshire County Council
County Hall, Walton Street, Aylesbury, HP20 1UA
☎ 01296 395000
✉ customerservices@buckscc.gov.uk
ⓘ www.buckscc.gov.uk

Buckinghamshire bus services
ⓘ www.buckscc.gov.uk/transport

City of London (Open Spaces Directorate)
Ashtead Estate Office, Woodfield Road, Ashtead, Surrey, KT21 2DU
☎ 01372 279083
ⓘ www.cityoflondon.gov.uk

Canal & Rivers Trust
4 Clarendon Road, Watford, WD17 1DA
☎ 0303 0404040
ⓘ www.canalrivertrust.org.uk

Epping Forest Visitor Centre
High Beach, Loughton, IG10 4AF
☎ 020 8508 0028
✉ epping.forest@cityoflondon.gov.uk
ⓘ www.cityoflondon.org.uk

Essex County Council
County Hall, Market Road, Chelmsford, CM1 1QH
☎ 0345 743 0430
✉ contact@essex.gov.uk
ⓘ www.essex.gov.uk

Essex bus services
ⓘ www.cartogold.co.uk/essex-public-transport

Hertfordshire County Council
County Hall, Pegs Lane, Hertford, SG13 8DQ
☎ 0300 123 4040
ⓘ www.hertfordshire.gov.uk

Hertfordshire bus services
ⓘ www.intalink.org.uk

London Wildlife Trust
Dean Bradley House, 52 Horseferry Road, London, SW1P 2AF
☎ 020 7261 0447
✉ enquiries@wildlondon.org.uk
ⓘ www.wildlondon.org.uk

National Trust
PO Box 574, Manvers, Rotherham,
S63 3FH
☎ 0344 800 1895
✉ enquiries@nationaltrust.org.uk
✆ www.nationaltrust.org.uk

National Rail Enquiries
☎ 03457 484950
✆ www.nationalrail.co.uk

Open Spaces Society
25 Bell Street, Henley-on-Thames,
RG9 2BA
☎ 01491 573535
✉ hq@os.org.uk
✆ www.oss.org.uk

Ordnance Survey
Explorer House, Adanac Drive,
Southampton, SO16 0AS
☎ 0345 605 0505
✆ www.ordnancesurvey.co.uk

The Ramblers
2nd Floor, Camelford House, 87 Albert
Embankment, London, SE1 7TW
☎ 020 7339 8500
✉ ramblers@ramblers.org.uk
✆ www.ramblers.org.uk

Surrey County Council
County Hall, Penrhyn Road,
Kingston-upon-Thames, KT1 2DN
☎ 03456 009009
✉ contact.centre@surreycc.gov.uk
✆ www.surreycc.gov.uk

Surrey bus services
✆ Via Surrey County Council website,
click 'Buses'

Thames Path National Trail
✆ www.nationaltrail.co.uk/thames-
path

Transport for London
☎ 0843 222 1234
✆ www.tfl.gov.uk/walking
🚇 https://tfl.gov.uk/plan-a-journey

Traveline
✆ www.travelinesoutheast.org.uk
For details of bus services outside
Greater London.

Tourist Information Centres

Bexley
Central Library, Townley Road,
Bexleyheath, DA6 7HJ
☎ 020 8303 7777, ask for Central
Library
✉ libraries.els@bexley.gov.uk

Kingston
Market House, Market Place,
Kingston-upon-Thames, KT1 1JS
☎ 020 8546 1140
✆ www.kingston.org.uk/tourist-
information

London
✆ www.visitlondon.com
Website includes list of tourist
information centres in London

Richmond
Civic Centre, 44 York Street,
Twickenham, TW1 3BZ
☎ 020 8891 1411
✆ www.visitrichmond.co.uk

The Grand Union Canal near Denham Lock.

Ordnance Survey maps covering the London Loop

Landranger maps (scale 1:50,000): sheets 176, 177 and 187.

Explorer maps (scale 1:25,000): sheets 162 Greenwich & Gravesend, 147 Sevenoaks & Tonbridge, 161 London South, 146 Dorking, Box Hill & Reigate, 160 Windsor, Weybridge & Bracknell, 172 Chiltern Hills East, 173 London North, 174 Epping Forest & Lea Valley, 175 Southend-on-Sea & Basildon.

Books and guides by the same author

The Capital Ring.
Aurum Press, 2016,
ISBN 9781781315699.
Companion route to the London Loop – a 125 km 'inner circle' walking route around London.

The North Downs Way.
Aurum Press, 2016,
ISBN 9781781315002.
A 245-km national trail from Farnham in Surrey to Dover in Kent.

Walking in the High Tatras.
Cicerone Press, 2017, ISBN tbc
A complete guide to walking in the Tatras mountains of Poland and Slovakia.

Rambling Away from 'The Smoke'.
Footline Press, 2014,
ISBN 9780992943400.
The history of the ramblers' excursions out of London 1932-2004.

The Strollerthon Story.
Footline Press, 2015,
ISBN 9780992943417
The history of a remarkable charity walk in London 1990-2001.

The Vanguard Way.
A 106-km walking route from Croydon to Newhaven. Free download from www.vanguardway.org.uk.

The Waymark Story.
The history of a remarkable tour operator specialising in walking and cross-country ski holidays. Free download from www.colinsaunders.org.uk.

The Official Guides to all o

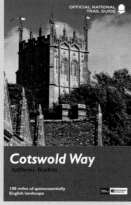

Cotswold Way
Anthony Burton

100 miles of quintessentially
English landscape

ISBN 978 1 84513 570 5

Cleveland Way
Ian Sampson

Over 100 miles of magnificent
walking on the North York Moors

ISBN 978 1 84513 781 6

Pennine Way
Damian Hall

268 miles, from the Peak District to Scotland:
Britain's oldest and toughest National Trail

ISBN 978 1 78131 565 1

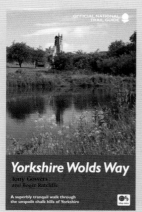

Yorkshire Wolds Way
Tony Gowers
and Roger Ratcliffe

A superbly tranquil walk through
the unspoilt chalk hills of Yorkshire

ISBN 978 178131 568 2

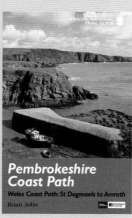

Pembrokeshire Coast Path
Wales Coast Path: St Dogmaels to Amroth
Brian John

ISBN 978 1 84513 782 3

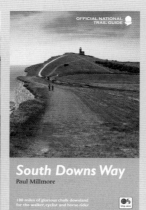

South Downs Way
Paul Millmore

100 miles of glorious chalk downland
for the walker, cyclist and horse rider

ISBN 978 1 78131 563 7

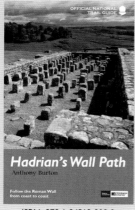

Hadrian's Wall Path
Anthony Burton

Follow the Roman Wall
from coast to coast

ISBN 978 1 84513 808 0

The Ridgeway
Anthony Burton

87 miles of downland walking
from Wiltshire to the Chilterns

ISBN 978 178131 063 2

North Downs Way
Colin Saunders

Follow the chalk ridge across South-East
England all the way to the sea

ISBN 978 178131 500 2

Britain's National Trails

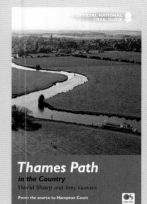

Thames Path
in the Country
David Sharp and Tony Gowers
From the source to Hampton Court

ISBN 978 1 78131 575 0

Thames Path
in London
Phoebe Clapham
From Hampton Court to Crayford Ness:
50 miles of historic riverside walk

ISBN 978 1 78131 574 3

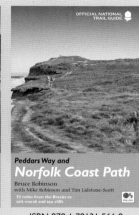

Peddars Way and
Norfolk Coast Path
Bruce Robinson
with Mike Robinson and Tim Lidstone-Scott
92 miles from the Brecks to
salt marsh and sea cliffs

ISBN 978 1 78131 566 8

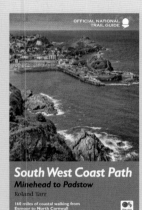

South West Coast Path
Minehead to Padstow
Roland Tarr
160 miles of coastal walking from
Exmoor to North Cornwall

ISBN 978 178131 564 4

South West Coast Path
Padstow to Falmouth
John Macadam
From golden beaches to rugged coves
around Britain's southernmost tip

ISBN 978 178131 062 5

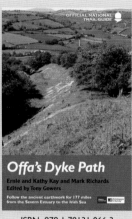

Offa's Dyke Path
Ernie and Kathy Kay and Mark Richards
Edited by Tony Gowers
Follow the ancient earthwork for 177 miles
from the Severn Estuary to the Irish Sea

ISBN 978 1 78131 066 3

South West Coast Path
Falmouth to Exmouth
Brian Le Messurier
172 miles of dramatic coves, cliffs and
beaches from Cornwall to Devon

ISBN 978 1 78131 486 9

South West Coast Path
Exmouth to Poole
Roland Tarr
From Jane Austen's Cobb to Lulworth Cove
– over 100 miles of historic coastline

ISBN 978 178131 567 5

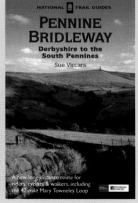

NATIONAL TRAIL GUIDES
PENNINE BRIDLEWAY
Derbyshire to the
South Pennines
Sue Viccars
A new long-distance route for
riders, cyclists & walkers, including
the 47-mile Mary Towneley Loop

ISBN 1 85410 957 X

Other guide books from Aurum Press

The Capital Ring
Colin Saunders

78 miles of green corridor
encircling inner London

ISBN 978 1 78131 569 9

The London Loop
Colin Saunders

150 miles of secret countryside to walk
in a green corridor around London

ISBN 978 1 78131 561 3

West Highland Way
Anthony Burton

94 miles of Scottish moor and
mountain in Britain's most
spectacular long-distance walk

ISBN 978 1 78131 576 7

The Coast to Coast Walk
Martin Wainwright

The classic high-level walk
from Irish Sea to North Sea

ISBN 978 1 84513 560 6

Northumberland Coast Path
Roland Tarr

From the centre of Newcastle
to the Scottish border

ISBN 978 178131 562 0

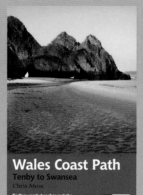

Wales Coast Path
Tenby to Swansea
Chris Moss

Endless sandy beaches and the
beautiful Gower Peninsula

ISBN 978 178131 067 0

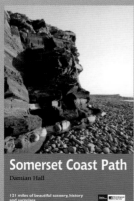

Somerset Coast Path
Damian Hall

121 miles of beautiful scenery, history
and surprises

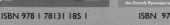

ISBN 978 1 78131 185 1

Camino de Santiago
Sergi Ramis

The ancient Way of Saint James pilgrimage route from
the French Pyrenees to Santiago de Compostela

ISBN 978 1 78131 223 0

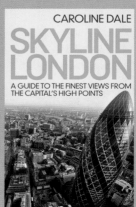

CAROLINE DALE

SKYLINE LONDON

A GUIDE TO THE FINEST VIEWS FROM
THE CAPITAL'S HIGH POINTS

ISBN 978 1 84513 762 5